I0126759

Sydney Chapman

Local government and state aid

An essay on the effect on local administration & finance of the payment to local

authorities of the proceeds of certain imperial taxes

Sydney Chapman

Local government and state aid
An essay on the effect on local administration & finance of the payment to local authorities of the proceeds of certain imperial taxes

ISBN/EAN: 9783337281403

Printed in Europe, USA, Canada, Australia, Japan

Cover: Foto ©Suzi / pixelio.de

More available books at **www.hansebooks.com**

LOCAL GOVERNMENT AND STATE AID

AN ESSAY ON THE EFFECT ON LOCAL ADMINISTRA-
TION AND FINANCE OF THE PAYMENT TO
LOCAL AUTHORITIES OF THE PROCEEDS
OF CERTAIN IMPERIAL TAXES

BY

SYDNEY J. CHAPMAN, M.A. (Lond.), B.A. (Cantab.)

Scholar of Trinity College, Cambridge ;
Lecturer in Political Science in the University College of South
Wales and Monmouthshire

LONDON
SWAN SONNENSCHEIN & CO., LIM.
PATERNOSTER SQUARE
1899

PREFACE

THIS essay, which was awarded the prize under the Warburton Trust by the Owens College, Manchester, at the beginning of the present year, was originally written in the long vacation of 1897. It has since been revised and expanded, and, wherever necessary, brought up to date. It is, nevertheless, issued very much in its original form, with those defects in proportion which can hardly be avoided when discussion is directed to a special subject implying portions of two sciences which are still fields for controversy. Whenever the treatment appears light-handed, the reader is asked to believe that it is due, in some degree, to the writer's fear of being carried far, and for long, from the special subject of the essay.

The author desires to express his great obligations to Prof. A. W. Flux for many valuable criticisms and suggestions: and, further, to thank Mr. K. T. S. Dockray for his careful reading of the proofs.

S. J. C.

THE OWENS COLLEGE,
MANCHESTER, *June*, 1899.

CONTENTS

CHAP.   PAGE

I. INTRODUCTORY - - - - -   I

II. DISTRIBUTION OF WORK BETWEEN LOCAL AND CENTRAL GOVERNMENTS - - -   4

III. THE DISTRIBUTION OF COST, AND THE GROUNDS FOR SUBVENTIONS TO LOCAL BODIES -   18

IV. THE LIMITED TAXING CAPACITIES OF LOCAL GOVERNMENTS - - - -   26

V. THE INCIDENCE, BURDEN, AND INEQUITIES OF THE RATES, AND POSSIBILITIES OF REFORM   37

VI. DIFFERENTIAL RATES AND THEIR CAUSES -   66

VII. SUBVENTIONS IN ENGLAND PRIOR TO 1888. -   88

VIII. THE SUBVENTION IN ENGLAND OF 1888 AND 1890 - - - - - -   94

IX. THE AGRICULTURAL RATINGS BILL - -   112

X. SUMMARY AND CONCLUSION - - -   120

APPENDIX A. THE EFFECT OF SUBVENTIONS ON THE QUANTITY AND INCIDENCE OF TAXATION - - - - - -   123

STATISTICAL APPENDICES - - - -   129

LOCAL GOVERNMENT AND STATE AID

CHAPTER I

INTRODUCTORY

A PRELIMINARY sketch of the plan of argument will be of assistance to the reader. Chapter I. deals with the relations with respect to governmental work between the central and the sectional governing bodies in the State. These relations are seen to involve various kinds of financial relations, which are further defined and reduced to principles in Chapter III. In Chapter III. also an *a priori* solution of the problem of subventions, to serve as a first guide to practical judgment, is offered ; but it is pointed out that the *a priori* scheme must be modified by the results of an *a posteriori* investigation, that, in a word, it is not a bed of Procrustes to which actual conditions are to be fitted, but a magic jacket to suit all comers.

The acceptance of the simple solution offered in

A

the provisional abstract determination is prevented
mainly by two allegations. The one, that socio-
logical conditions are such that local bodies are
impotent as taxing authorities. This assertion ne-
cessitated an investigation in Chapter IV. into the
possible range of local taxes, and, when the necessary
predominance of the one-tax system was demonstrated, an examination in Chapter V. of its equities,
which embraced, of course, some discussion of the
incidence of rates. The other, that differential rates
imply differential burdens, which should imply
differential subventions. Chapter VI. was given
over to a minute scrutiny of the grounds for this
statement.

In the light of the conclusions adopted on all the
foregoing topics, the various subventions which are,
or have been, existent in England and Wales are
criticised in Chapters VII., VIII., and IX ; and in
Chapter VIII. the excuse that local governments had
to be stimulated in some manner is treated also,
together with other small contentions. Chapter X.
shortly sums the argument, and attempts a practical
conclusion.

There, in brief, is a description of what some might
term a Nasmyth hammer to crack a filbert. The
extent of the argument, however, may be justified
from two directions. In the first place, the question
of subventions is perhaps more momentous than it at
first appears. There are those who so regard it. In

the second place, that which is worth calling extraneous to any subject is generally highly relevant.

One word must be said in explanation of the method adopted, especially in Chapters II. and III. By trying to avoid the errors of the over-starched philosophy of the middle-century dogmatists I have been driven into a somewhat free use of the biological analogy, without any of that careful definition and limitation which is so necessary to its fruitful employment. The sole excuse for the absence of explanations is contracted space. If the treatment here offered prove suggestive I am content that it is not exhaustive or quite exact.

Quite apart from the main argument directed against subventions, the chapters of this book may be read as separate essays on some of the important political, economic, and financial problems arising out of local government.

CHAPTER II

DISTRIBUTION OF WORK BETWEEN LOCAL AND CENTRAL GOVERNMENTS

ALL western countries have a more or less developed system of division of governmental labour.[1] England has the County, the County Borough, the Urban and Rural Districts; the United States the State and the County; Prussia the Province, the Circle and the District; France the Department, the Arrondissement and the Canton; and all have the primitive cell, the Parish, or Township, or Commune.

Division of labour and distribution of labour, whether in matters of production or in matters of government, are distinct things. Division of labour, to use the term in the sense in which it was employed by Adam Smith, is only one of the methods of arranging work.

How does this method of distributing labour arise? Adam Smith set himself to answer the question, for it apparently seemed to him remarkable that in a society built upon the individuality of the individual

[1] " Governmental labour" is used throughout this work, in the broadest possible sense, of any state functions and municipal activities, of whatever kind.

men should come together and organise their labour. Enlightened self-interest, he seemed to think, was not sufficient to account for the destruction of the self-sufficiency, the instinctive self-supporting policy, of the individual. The cause, he says, is an instinct.

The further study of biology and sociology confirms the hint thrown out by Adam Smith. Prof. Marshall is of opinion that recent researches have indicated "a fundamental unity of action between the laws of nature in the physical and in the moral world. This central unity is set forth in the general rule, to which there are very many exceptions, that the development of the organism, whether social or physical, involves greater subdivision of functions between its separate parts on the one hand, *and on the other a more intimate connection between them.*" [1] (The italics are mine.)

In other words, from one point of view, society is an organic whole, and its end is a determinant of the organisation of labour (whether industrial or governmental) within it. One explanation, then, of social organisation lies in the organic nature of society, as the new title "organisation" for an old conception, as old as Plato at least, implies. To speak in analogy, the local body must be conceived as an organism within an organism. A developed society is a vital unity built up in an hierarchy of organically related organisms. Special emphasis should be given to the

[1] "Principles of Economics," 2nd ed., p. 300.

term "hierarchy." We have around us more than groups of organisms with distinct and independent functions and scopes of operation. We have a system in which it is the function of the higher organism to see to the adequate functioning of the lower organisms ; in other words, a system in which it is a special function of the higher centre to stimulate, organise and supervise the general functioning of the lower centres. If it were not so the nation, consisting of groups of localities, could not be correctly viewed as a unity.

The conception of the hierarchically constituted organism must be elucidated further, for it is a notion of importance to this investigation. We frequently hear local government contrasted with central government ; but we seldom hear tell of the problem of the intermediate governments lying between the two. Yet there are such ; and their position has been one of much prominence since 1888. They will be termed " provincial governments," or " county governments," hereafter, when it is sought to distinguish them from the primary local polities, to which also a special term, " district governments," will be applied, when it is desired to summon attention to the primitive political cell.

A developed western people seems to be invariably drawn by the bonds of civic feeling into formations somewhat like those indicated in the following scheme :

1. The Locality: a political organism.

(*a*) The District or Parish : a simple political organism : part of a larger whole, and a whole itself, but not of parts.

(*b*) The Province or County : a complex political organism : part of a larger whole, and a whole of parts.

2. The Nation : a complex organism in its ultimate form : a whole of parts, but not part of a larger whole.[1]

Of course, this analogical scheme is not meant to imply that the government of the complex organism is related to other political organisms only ; that it is not directly constituted by the suffrages of individuals, and that it does not directly govern individuals. It may take many forms, from the federal council of political bodies acting only through those bodies, to the popularly elected county council with its duties of both direct and indirect government. Nor do I mean to assert that existing local governments, always or generally, correspond in structure and function to those which reason proposes.

The importance of strongly-developed local governments can hardly be over-emphasised.

As national character determines these bodies, so do these bodies react on character. Local govern-

---

[1] This is not quite true, because international law just hints at a gradually segregating higher organism.

ment stimulates and educates the political interests
of a people, and with political interests the char-
acteristics of self-reliance, vigour, and enterprise. The
direct effect is political, but the indirect includes
almost all social and individual qualities. Over-
centralisation of government means a slack and
ineffective control on the part of the constituents,
and it increases the risk of storms of unreasonable
discontent and unreasoning excitement.

Moreover the over-loading of the central government with work clogs its action and so reduces its
efficiency. The future of representative government
—and in this is involved the future of civilisation—
is wrapped up in the future of local self-government.

In seeking to define the scope of local governments, we are immediately and forcibly struck by the
fact, indicated in the preceding analysis, that the local
body may be conceived in two apparently mutually
exclusive ways, as a whole and as a part. It is at
the same time an organism and the limb of an
organism, which again may be a part in relation to a
higher unity. The perplexity which naturally
accompanies such a discovery is by no means
decreased when the implications of the dual nature
force their way to the surface. It is not long before
we clearly perceive that the two aspects of the local
body lead to two principles for the sub-division
of governing powers, and that the two principles

do not necessarily unite in the same thing at the end. Let us now consider each principle and its results.

1. The local body as individual must be self-governing. Adam Smith makes this notion the central pivot of "the obvious and simple system of natural liberty." It is the citadel of individualism. Admitting the force of the contention, we are bound to accept the following principle: *Of the matters which fall within the scope of government, those which are chiefly of local interest must be undertaken by the corresponding local governments, and those which are chiefly of national interest must be undertaken by the central government.*

In comparing the distribution of work in the two spheres of politics and industry, we must remember that in the former there are no markets, and that, therefore, there is in it no competition to force the greatest efficiency at the least cost. Hence the special importance of the individualistic principle of self-sufficiency in politics. Manchester and Liverpool cannot in the nature of things strive with one another for the management of, say, the police in either town, even assuming a desire on the part of both to do the Empire's work. In each case the sole possibilities by way of management consist in arrangements between the imperial executive and the city's government; in each case all other governments are foreign to the matter.

But there are exceptions. For instance, in the matter of the chief constableship of Suffolk, the Home Secretary decided this year in favour of the claim of West Suffolk to appoint its own chief constable, and against the joint standing committee, which aspired to make the appointment for the whole county.

2. The local body as the limb of an organism, that is, as part only of an individual, must do that kind of work for which it is most adapted. This conception gives rise to the following principle : *The matters which fall within the scope of government must be distributed among the various governing bodies, central and local, according to their capacities and efficiencies.*

These are the two main principles for the distribution of work among governing bodies. It need not be added that the second is a particular form of that which used to be known as the Principle of the Division of Labour. In its modern dress it might be known as the Principle of Socialism. The Principle of Individualism would not be a serious misnomer for the first.

The two principles are equally true. In all cases we have to appeal to both ; neither must be pushed to an extreme ; but no rule can be laid down as to the weight to be attached to each. Resultant advantages, which, of course, depend on notions of the social ideal, determine the applicability of each.

Though there are cases in which the one alone seems called for, the other must always be held in mind.

By the aid of the above principles, and in the light of the foregoing discussion, we may now attempt in more detail the design of the distribution of governmental function, bearing in mind, however, that deduction can only rudely sketch, and that wide experience alone has the power to paint in the detail; and remembering also that the conclusions below follow not from the bare principles, but from the relative emphasis laid upon each.

A first rough apportionment of work may be based on the distinction between matters of purely national and those of purely local interest. Thus, the question of national security may be held to be a purely national one, and the position and administration of naval and military forces may, therefore, be relegated to the central government. More widely, all concerns of external policy must be handed over to the central government, while matters of purely local interest, inasmuch as they concern only their locality, may well be left to local management; indeed, it would be difficult to find a principle by which central interference in the latter case could be justified. There are, however, no such cases; always the nation as a whole is in some degree affected by local policy. It is therefore desirable—unless, indeed, it be held that it is better that unitary states should fall asunder into confederacies, the locality becoming the prime unit in place of the nation as a whole—that the central government should limit the scope of local governmental function by regulation and by general supervision. In many departments, nevertheless, great latitude may be safely allowed to local bodies.

In spite of the above contentions, however, it is possible, for all practical purposes, to separate matters of national from those of chiefly local importance ; but even when the divorce has been effected, the problem of the relation between central and local authorities is by no means completely solved. There remain those matters which at the same time substantially affect both the nation as a whole and the localities. To refer for the present only to the governmental functions included in the "Individualistic Minimum" theory of politics, there are affairs of justice and police. Security and the wise and impartial administration of justice are of vital importance to the localities; but the nation as a whole cannot be indifferent to the provisions for the attainment of these objects. It is of special concern to a town that the detection of crime should be swift and sure, and the positive prevention of crime as frequent as possible; and it is of great concern to the community at large that no district should become a hotbed of vice. On the one hand, therefore, there are strong arguments for relegating matters of justice and police to local control ; and, on the other hand, there are strong arguments for centralised authority.

When we pass beyond the narrow confines of Individualistic Politics we find that matters of an appreciable dualistic interest are common, *e.g.*, those of the poor, of pauper lunatics, of sanitation, education, bridges, and highways. Take the question of the poor as an example. Poor relief, from the "Settlement" of Elizabeth to 1834, was almost entirely district business. The cost was colossal, and the unnecessary effort expended was simply monstrous. "Domicile" or "settlement" became a constant subject of dispute. The good work done by one parish was frequently undone by inefficient administration in the next. Incapable boards peopled the country with paupers. The nation suffered, the deserving poor suffered, and none, except, perhaps, the able-bodied and idle vagabonds, profited. There is, notwithstanding, no reason to suppose that purely central management would have prospered better. No matter requires more patient examination of detail, more minute supervision and local knowledge, than poor relief; and in all these respects the central government is defective.

It is unnecessary to enter into detail with regard to the other affairs of divided interest set forth above. They will all be found on a brief inspection to exhibit elements which specially fit them for determination by the central government, and, at the same time, elements which mark them off as the natural business of local bodies. But of which local bodies?

We must here refer back for a few moments to the conception of the nation as an hierarchy of social bodies. Among developed western peoples we find not only central and district governments, but also intermediate governments lying between the two extremes. The last are of considerable importance. For one reason, because *the intensity of interest in matters of divided interest diminishes in all cases with distance from the locality where the work is performed.* Take an example. Efficient policing in Manchester is of almost equal importance to the urban districts lying about it as to the city itself, and it is of much importance to southern and central Lancashire; while its interest to Devon is something infinitesimal in comparison. This fact will form the basis of many of our conclusions as to subventions. In dealing with the intermediate or county governments, however, we must always remember that there are differences between their relations to the districts beneath them and the relations of the nation to the localities. The control of the county over the district is strictly curtailed by the fact that the closer bodies lie together in the scale of government the more friction does control induce, and the more effective is it in degrading the quality of the subordinate board.

So far we have been concerned chiefly with the local or national interest attaching to certain operations. Now we have to notice more especially the division of function determined by the nature of the governmental organs. Each has its particular gifts. In general we may say that the matters assigned to local bodies should be those in which local knowledge is requisite, minute supervision essential, and the co-operation of private and governmental agencies likely to be of appreciable value; and those in which the need for uniformity is least evident, or in which even diversity in administration is desirable. Some laws are not good if local peculiarities and differences are ignored in their application. Uniform administration is best only when local conditions are uniform or negligible. The administration of the Poor Laws may again be taken as an example. One can barely conceive a greater political mistake than detailed uniformity in the application of these laws—especially with respect to indoor and outdoor relief—in London, say, and in the rural districts of Devon, or in Essex, under the present cloud of agricultural depression.

Further, we must carefully guard against the mistake of supposing that the division of work between the national and the local governing organs is absolute, and quite independent of the quantity of work. In a word, that it is analagous to division of industrial labour within one country.

To repeat, many services are the direct concern of both the central and local bodies, and many largely of national interest may be best performed by the locality, either because of its idiosyncracies, or because of the peculiarities in certain districts, or because the central government has its hands full. Moreover, operations of special importance to the locality, and managed by the locality, may be improved if brought into contact with the central government. The position of the local government is one of tutelage. It is taught by advice, correction and example. To quote Prof. Sidgwick : "We have also to consider the probability that both the central government and its critics—as compared with local government and critics—will have the superior enlightenment derived from greater general knowledge, wider experience, and more highly-trained intellects ; and we have to consider the greater danger in a small locality that the sinister influence of a powerful individual or corporation, or combination of persons with similiar interests, may predominate to the detriment of the public." [1]

Finally, we must notice that local governments have a wonderful power of adapting themselves to circumstances. By undertaking a higher quality of work they attract to their boards higher ability. Hence difficult undertakings calling for tact, large knowledge, and perhaps some genius, which cannot at first be safely placed in the hands of local bodies without the most zealous supervision, may in a few years be wholly handed over to them with perfect confidence.

After the foregoing, Roscher's division of local

[1] "Elements of Politics," p. 514.

functions will be immediately comprehended. They are, he says,

(*a*) State.

(*b*) Compulsory.

(*c*) Optional.

The first class sets apart the local administration of centrally initiated services of chiefly national interest. The second class contains only matters of divided interest. Of these we may remark again that the division of interest rests very largely between the provinces and districts. The third class comprises those concerns which are specifically local.

Lastly, it has to be kept vividly before the mind that the so-called local organism is constituted by function ; that the aggregation of human beings which may be regarded as bound into a whole by civic feeling for one purpose may not be so regarded for another purpose. That the size and strength of the local organism varies with its activities ; and moreover that the cohesion of its parts becomes less firm with increasing distance from the centre.

CHAPTER III

THE DISTRIBUTION OF COST, AND THE GROUNDS FOR SUBVENTIONS TO LOCAL BODIES

AFTER dwelling for some time upon the question of the distribution of cost, we discover fold upon fold of further complications doubled over those which have already taxed our patience in the matter of the distribution of work. Just as we learnt then that not only one but several principles, co-operating and competing, existed for the distribution of governmental operations, so we learn now that not only one but several principles, co-operating and competing, exist for the distribution of costs. The chief are the following :—

1. *Ethical Principles.*

(*a*) *Those interested should bear the cost, and in proportion to their interests.*

(*b*) *The burden of cost should be distributed according to ability to bear it.*

The former emphasises the indestructible individuality both of the locality and of the nation as a whole ; the latter the transcending of the mere individuality of the section by the unity of the whole body corporate.

Now to which principle we give precedence—to the other being accorded only the office of limitation —depends upon the priority of the individualities with which we are dealing. In states approximating to confederacies, the first is the fundamental rule, but in those more closely resembling unitary bodies politic the second has the superior claim. Frequently it does not much matter with which we commence, but in England to-day, in view of the importance and the ancient foundation of the local bodies, it will doubtless be best to apply first the ethical principle based upon their individuality.

2. *The Economic Principle.*

Those who carry out the work should reap advantages varying with their economy.

The necessity is immediately obvious. That nobody is so careful in spending other people's money as in spending his own is a psychological fact.

These are the fundamental rules, but they form only part of the frame-work of principles for guidance in distributing costs. Here are others of secondary importance.

3. *The Juridical Principle.*

Costs, or some portion of them, should be used as legal sanctions to enforce control.

In an hierarchy of polities there must obviously be

some control by the head over the lower centres, and practically it is only by the financial method that one corporation can effectively coerce another.

4. *The Political Principle.*

Costs, or some portion of them, should be employed as a political regulator, by means of which the activities of local governments may be stimulated or checked.

And this is not quite all, for, by the principle of Division of Labour, those bodies which can perform that delicate office best ought to collect the funds for political operations.

The last principle is strictly subordinate to all which precede, when it conflicts with them, which it is sometimes said to do so directly and completely as to place the hostility almost beyond reach of compromise. The prior rules must be observed first, and then, if it is found that there are substantial differences in the powers of different bodies to raise economically and equitably the requisite funds, modifications must be built in, to obviate the incidental disadvantages attaching to the arrangements most in accordance with the dominating principles.

Many as they are, the principles before us are not exhaustive. Overshadowing all, hangs the great rule of simplicity. We gain frequently by retaining defects to avoid complexities. The more involved are mechanical and social arrangements, the more intricate are the relations between units of any

character in combination, the greater is the friction
and incidental loss, the greater the chance of disloca-
tion and breakdown. The higher the state of development, the safer and more economical do the
more delicate and complicated sub-divisions in
organisation become ; but limits are set to the
practicability of theoretical schemes at each stage of
development.

Let us now attempt to apply the foregoing principles to the financial problems which arise from the
distribution of governmental work treated in the
second chapter. For the present, the obligation on
the part of the Imperial Government to play the part
of Providence to the local bodies is best ignored.

We may at once lay it down that State functions
performed by the State must be paid for by the
State, and that optional functions undertaken by the
locality must be paid for by the locality.

And who should bear the costs of (*a*) State
functions effected in part by the locality, and (*b*)
compulsory functions ?

One of the weightiest problems to which we have
been converging is before us. It need not be added
that of the solutions given in the past subventions in
great variety, doles, loans, sops, and part payments
form by far the largest number. The following I
take to be the main lines of a rational solution :

State Functions.—They should be paid for by the
State. But, to enforce economy, definite prices should

be fixed. What difference there is between them and the actual costs should belong to, or be met by, the locality. Payment must be conditional upon the attainment of some standard of excellence; and where possible, it may be desirable to vary it, within limits, with the quality of the work done.

Compulsory Functions.—Most of them may be considered as in small part State, in large part provincial, and in largest part district functions; the proportions being determined by relative interests. The hardest task lies in estimating the proportions of interest; in drawing a line where nature has made no division. Suppose the question settled, however. Assume, for instance, that, as regards a particular piece of work—say, education—experience has shown that outside funds ought to bear about one-quarter of the expense. Then contributions to the cost of administration, roughly upon this basis, must observe the rules laid down with respect to payments for State functions. Definite prices must be fixed, dependent upon efficiency, and varying, perhaps, within limits, with the quality of the work done.

Here a thought intrudes which calls for some limitations. Suppose that each locality contributes to the imperial exchequer through the medium of imperial taxes, for the purpose of meeting the cost of the localities' State and compulsory functions, just as much as it receives from the exchequer for the performance of these functions; then the paying and paying back is clearly absurd. If such were the case, the sole principles determining contribution would be the third and fourth. We shall have to investigate in succeeding chapters whether such is the case.

The obligation on the part of the central government to stimulate the localities on occasion raises grave issues. It may be taken as pretty generally true that the use of a stimulus implies an ignorance —an ignorance either of the quantity of vitality in the body, corporeal or corporate, or of some disease which has insinuated itself. It is hoped that activity will add to the vitality or drive out the disease ; at any rate it is intended that the body shall at least act as if it were in a healthy condition. Thus, when a man's vitality is yielding, he may keep himself vigorous with brandy, and a fagged horse may be urged to greater speed by whip and spur. But stimuli must increase in something like a geometrical progression to achieve a moderately constant result, and even then they secure it only for a short period, provided that the obstacle impeding vitality has not been detected and removed, and generally at the cost of greatly impaired health. A stimulus of the kind we are considering, then, must be only temporarily applied, if at all, and it must be accompanied by a searching analysis of the constitution of the body stimulated ; even the temporary starting stimulus is undesirable, because it tends to destroy initiative. We shall observe hereafter that in politics the tem-

porary measure has a powerful proclivity to establish-
ing itself permanently.

What nature should the stimuli to local authorities
assume, supposing them to be on occasion really
essential political expedients? In the first place they
must be financial in character. Other peculiarities
depend upon the ends which they are intended to sub-
serve. If it is held that a certain sort of work should be
done by healthy local bodies, then it is best to pay a
bonus on its performance till the locality has acquired
the habit of doing it. When this consummation is
attained the special stimulus must be removed ; and
the cost of the work must thereafter be met in accordance with the prior principles. If the local body
persistently refuses to acquire the desired habit, then
the local performance of the work and the subvention
must cease together. If it is desired simply to stir
up the local body, then, overlooking the dangers and
granting the expediency of that which is contem-
plated, it is wise not to assume certain costs, since
that simply means paying some old bills, but to hand
over a lump sum, and to vary it occasionally to keep
the recipients alive to their financial problems.

The preceding is an entirely deductive solution of
the problem underlying the policy of subventions.
Actual subventions cannot be approved or condemned without a knowledge of actual conditions.

The following are some of the questions which

must be faced before a practical judgment can be formed :

Can local bodies raise the funds they require as economically and equitably as the Imperial Government ? Do they ? If not, is the difference sufficient to justify special financial arrangements to meet it ?

Does the wealth of local constituencies vary much from place to place ? If so, should the outside contributions to the cost of compulsory functions vary in any way with the resources of the locality ? Does poverty justify special assistance ?

Is there much difference between the costs of " state functions " and " compulsory functions " in different districts ? Should such differences, if existent, regulate the amount of outside contributions ?

Is the question of the cost of compulsory functions adequately met by financial arrangements between districts and the county within which they lie, or are some exchequer contributions needful ?

Has there been anything in the condition of local self-government in recent years to render a special financial stimulus desirable ? Is it desirable now ?

These questions will be answered in what follows as fully as space and information permit, and the requirements of the subject render indispensable, and in the order which commends itself as most appropriate.

CHAPTER IV

THE LIMITED TAXING CAPACITIES OF LOCAL GOVERNMENTS

IT does on first thoughts seem extraordinary that the Imperial Government should have an almost infinite choice of means for tapping the wealth of the country, that it should use dozens, and that the local governments should be confined to practically one only tax; especially in view of the fact that the one-tax system is defective because of its oneness; although much can be said for it. Can local finance escape the one-tax system?

In modern civilised states many forms of taxation possible to the central government are impossible to local bodies.

Customs, for instance, can only be levied at the frontiers of a state. Local bodies, therefore, are interdicted from that form of taxation. We find, indeed, octrois in many continental European countries; but they differ from customs in being levied alike on home and foreign goods. Octrois, moreover, are on the wane, as the opinion is gaining ground that the results are not worth the annoyance caused by collection, the cost of collection, and the impediments to trade which are wrapped up in the system. With a few exceptions, for instance in Italy and France, they have already been commuted for fixed payments. This form of taxation, however, bears a closer resemblance to an impost upon consumption than to customs.

Excise duties are likewise closed to local authorities. The reason is that sectional governments have no control over one another and over the customs, and so, if they imposed excise duties, the local producer might be ruthlessly sacrificed, with the best intentions in the world. Stamps on business and legal documents fall also within the classes of taxes from which localities are debarred. General supervision from Westminster would prevent such a disaster in some degree, but probably at a cost that would swallow up any little advantage. Nor could much efficiency be expected in any central organisation and supervision. The probablity, therefore, is that had the local bodies powers to impose these taxes, trade, tossed into an atmosphere of insecurity, would be subjected to arbitrarily induced convulsions.

The two chief forms of indirect taxation are, therefore, weapons not fashioned to the grasp of local bodies. We shall find, moreover, that the scope of direct taxation in their hands is substantially contracted.

Of the direct taxes, those on income and property first claim attention. The former cannot be better introduced than by a quotation from Mr. Goschen's report :—" It appears to be impossible to devise an equitable local income tax, for you cannot localise income. An attempt was made in Scotland, and it broke down when an English Lord Chancellor, who drew his £10,000 a year in London, but had a small place in Scotland, was made to pay income tax on the whole of his income in that country as well as in this. No country has been able to levy a local income tax."[1] I see no fatal objection in the double payment of the income tax by those who keep up two residential establishments; and business establishments might be specially treated. The subject taxed more than once might be charged at a lower rate, the double imposition being employed in rendering taxation degressive. But a very real obstacle does exist in the fact that a great mass of English income is taxed at its source. If it were not, the opportunities for fraud would be enormous, and experience shows that they would not all be wasted. The plan of stoppage at the source was not included in the first income tax imposed by Pitt in 1799, and the results were disappointing. The tax was repeated three years later, and Pitt complained bitterly of the frauds by which contribution had been evaded. When Addington reimposed the tax in 1803 it was col-

[1] "Report on Local Taxation," p. 204.

lected at the source whenever possible. Relative
productivity was at once doubled as a direct consequence, notwithstanding the imperfections of the new
method at the outset. Professor Bastable's judgment may be taken as final :—" Owing to the variety
of modern incomes and the trouble of following them
to their source, the income tax should always be a
general tax."[1]

In Switzerland and the United States the general
property tax is the main instrument for providing the
revenue of the component parts of the federal system.
Prussia and Holland have recently reverted to it.
The tax is, however, almost universally condemned
because of the gigantic difficulty in the way of equitable administration, and of the fact that fraud can be
practised with almost complete immunity from detection. The tax comes in consequence to fall for
the most part on real property, the least tangible
possessions remaining undeclared and undiscovered.
Mr. D. A. Wells concludes that the property tax is a
scandalous fraud. Professor Seligman considers it
the worst known tax in the civilised world. Professor
Plehn condemns it in unmeasured terms :—" As at
present administered, it fails entirely to reach in-
tangible property. It debases public morals by
putting a premium on dishonesty. It is regressive,
and presses hardest upon those relatively least able
to pay. This is strong language; even stronger has

[1] "Public Finance," p. 360.

been used. But no words are too strong to express the iniquities of this tax."[1]

Yet the opinion frequently crops up, and is frequently expressed in popular debate, that local bodies should relieve the rates by a property tax. Notice the dilemma which such a tax creates. It is either grossly unfair, and offers a big bounty on fraud, or else the individual must be subjected to exasperating interferences, and society must be exposed to the damaging effects of inquisitorial investigation. This dilemma applies also to a local income tax; and the objections to a local income tax, put forward by Mr. Goschen in the passage quoted above, apply with equal force to a local property tax.

Against the foregoing general analysis it may be urged that the independence of local finance is not universal. In France, for instance, local funds are chiefly raised by the imposition of *centimes additionels* on some of the imperial taxes. The local tax thus becomes a mere appendage to the imperial tax. This method of raising local funds has the cordial support of M. P. Leroy-Beaulieu on the grounds of clearness, simplicity, economy, and security against peculation and exaction. But the system simply means that imperial taxes must be innoculated with the infirmities of local taxes in being collected only direct from the localities; or else that the local taxes must be collected on the basis of part only of the

[1] Plehn's " Introduction to the Science of Finance," p. 219.

imperial taxes—which is actually the case—so that the question of the scope of each remains. Further, the *additionel* method, by robbing local bodies of a certain amount of initiative, undermines anything of the nature of robust independence.

Here a very serious difficulty confronts us. We referred in the first chapter to the overlapping of governmental bodies; we have now to observe an overlapping on the financial side. The imperial government may draw its income from all the taxes above noted; the local bodies derive their revenues from a portion of them. The disadvantages attendant on financial overlapping are considerable. It is quite obvious that if two bodies have the power of taxing on the same base neither will be governed by considerations of the taxable capacity of that particular base. If two costers possess a donkey in common it will be overworked, for each man will argue, "If I do not overwork this animal my partner in ownership will; if I regard economic and humane considerations I shall lose and it will not gain, for there is no guarantee that my partner will do the same." And so it will be with the base controlled by two taxing authorities. And even if we suppose that Her Majesty's Government will see to it that no single tax runs riot, yet there are fatal objections. Suppose the centre only taxed to the amount of the difference between the local rate (confined perhaps within limits) and the maximum which that base should

bear in the taxing system. Then a powerful check
on wastefulness on the part of a local body would be
withdrawn ; for however high or low its rates the
constituency would neither suffer nor benefit (the
imperial tax varying inversely as the local tax).
Each local body would strive to raise its taxes as
high as was allowable, and its constituents would
applaud, for heavy expenditure would simply mean
that the locality was sucking the wealth of the nation
at large. The central government, indeed, might
supervise local taxes, but by so doing it would sap
the initiative of local bodies and run the risk of all
the dangers of over centralisation. Other ways out
of the difficulty have been found in the suggestions
that the common base should be divided, or that the
central body should take it over entirely and pay to
the local authorities a portion of the proceeds—the
additionel system again. In the United Kingdom,
for example, by the Act of 1888, certain licenses collected in any county or county borough are paid to
the authorities of those localities.[1]

[1] The licenses thus transferred are those for the sale of in-
toxicating liquors by retail for consumption on or off the
premises, licenses for dealers in beer, spirits, wine, sweets,
tobacco, and game, for refreshment-house keepers, appraisers,
auctioneers, hawkers, house-agents, pawnbrokers and plate-
dealers, dog, gun and carriages licenses, and licenses for killing
game, and for armorial bearings, and male servants. It was
originally intended to add the sum which might be collected on
certain licenses for trade-carts, locomotives, etc., which it was
proposed to authorise by a bill which was before Parliament

It may be argued against their proposed uncon-
ditional surrender to sectional governments that uniformity is essential, since trade would be hampered
by differential burdens especially if they were variable. But really this objection becomes slight when
we consider what the licenses are. The same contention holds also with respect to rates on business
premises; but it does not apply to consumers' licenses,
nor to liquor licenses, and these are, therefore, specially
suitable for local manipulation. The local bodies
cannot in the face of the rates reduce them, and no
considerable harm could result from a large increase
in them. A very obvious fact which vitiates the
present system is that, unless responsibility in spending funds is accompanied by responsibility in finding
them, there is the risk of preventing anything
satisfactory emerging.

The base consisting in land and buildings should be
entirely yielded up to the localities. This once almost
ceased to be a pressing need. In 1871 Mr. Goschen
had a bill drafted, to apply to England only, in
which the following clause occurred :—" From and
after a certain date, to be fixed by an order in Council,

at the time of the passing of the Act. On the whole the proposal was a good one, as part of the cost of making and repairing streets should be considered as an element in the cost
of production and circulation of goods, and should be charged
in the price of those goods in proportion to the amount of
transporting involved. There would be a difficulty however as
regards carts kept outside the rateable area.

C

the house tax shall cease to be payable to the
Crown, but shall be levied by and be payable to the
parochial board in each parish." The bill, however,
was finally dropped, and Mr. Goschen gave it as his
opinion that the time had not yet come for the
central government to surrender the house tax.
Certainly the time had not yet come if the Government decided to drop the bill. But, whatever was
the case then, the time is more than fully ripe now
for the removal of this imperial tax, absurd as it
is in the face of rapidly-swelling rates. Not only
is its retention needless, unwise, and a standing
source of irritation, but it is simply scandalous in
face of the doles which Her Majesty's Government
have felt constrained to mete out to the localities in
the form of allocated taxes and other subventions.

Would an estate duty on real property be at all
suitable for local purposes ? It is needful of course
that any death duty relegated to sectional control
should be on realty, which can be localised, while
personal property cannot. The duties now paid into
the Local Taxation Accounts are based on personalty ; they are, therefore, in no sense local taxes. If
they were levied on realty they could be surrendered
to the local authorities, but the objection would then
hold that a taxation base was divided, and there are
grave disadvantages attaching to the transference to
local bodies for taxation purposes of the whole of
real property passing at death. Besides, realty and

personalty are so closely related that they form to a certain extent one base; and we may lay it down as a fundamental principle that no one base must fall within the control of two or more authorities.

To sum up, we find that district governments are curtailed in their choice of taxes principally because of—

(*a*) The need of uniformity in indirect taxation, and the requirement that certain imposts should be treated together.

(*b*) The fact that the individual and his capital pass more easily from district to district than from country to country.

In the society of Tennyson's ideal of a cosmopolitan democracy, the income tax will be as impossible to the nation as to the locality, since taxation at the source will be rendered futile by the international flow of capital—unless, indeed, people will then be eager to pay their taxes.

The one-tax system, we observe, is not in the nature of things compulsory. Local taxation may be expanded, but its co-efficient of expansion is small.

I am almost inclined to think that for the present no extension will be found necessary. We shall see hereafter that the apparent one-tax system is in reality a three-tax system. It is, moreover, doubtful whether existing local bodies are sufficiently capable to take over larger financial responsibilities; but it must be remembered that enlarged powers, by attracting more of the higher ability, lead to increased efficiency. There is, moreover, very much to be said for the one-tax system; it is simple, it is economical, it may be made equitable, and the increase or decrease in the expenditure of local bodies is thereby kept prominently before each citizen. Adam Smith emphasises this last element as desirable in a scheme of taxation. Without giving an unqualified assent to Adam Smith's dictum, I agree that this clearness is convenient now in matters of local finance. For though there are cases in which a wise increase in expenditure might be prevented by popular clamour, they are confined in largest part to affairs of imperial policy.

The scope of local taxation may be widened, but at its biggest stretch, in comparison with the possibilities of imperial taxation, it can be but a fly on the foot of a Colossus. It cannot touch most of the indirect taxes, because of the need of uniformity and for other reasons. It must, therefore, never hope to acquire such a mass of taxes that unintentional and unavoidable inequalities here and there will be shifted by the law of error.

The staple financial food of local governments must always be the rates.

This being so, we are bound to inquire next whether the failings accompanying the raising of local funds by rates are essential, or merely accidental and removeable, given the determination and strength to carry into effect local financial reforms.

CHAPTER V

THE INCIDENCE, BURDEN, AND INEQUITIES OF THE RATES, AND POSSIBILITIES OF REFORM

THE subject of this chapter is more important than that of the burden and incidence of a match-tax or of the stamp duties, or, in fact, of any other single tax. We might decide about them, that their incidence was only moderately equitable, and yet judge them desirable ; and we might yield to the temptation to give only rough estimates without doing much harm, because, after all, each of them is only one of many. But we may not do so in the case of the rates. They are practically the sole tax of any magnitude now open to local bodies ; and in consequence, their incidence means the incidence of all local taxation. They are, moreover, of colossal size, so that a mere fractional injustice may be a very heavy burden.

Consider for one moment the volume of the rates, with a view to some adequate appreciation of the pressing practical importance of our inquiry. The house duty is, of course, a rate which happens to be an imperial one, and one, moreover, which should have been given up long ago. Let us then add to the rates in the United Kingdom for 1893-4 the house duty for that year. The result is a sum of £50,095,212, collected mainly from occupiers. This is enormous. Some conception of the amount may be gained by comparing it with other great taxes in this country. Not one of them yielded half the sum in the same year, except the excise, which produced just over half, namely, £25,200,000. The income tax yielded £15,200,000, less than one-third of the sum raised by rates and the house tax ; and the customs only £19,707,000, less than two-fifths as much. Further, the total imperial net revenue was but £91,133,410 in the same year, a sum not twice as great by over nine millions.

Our object in this chapter is to discover whether the rates, fall where, and in the manner in which, accepted principles of taxation declare they ought to fall. What the English occupier sees in the rates is that he pays them, and that after paying them he is the poorer by exactly their amount. What he does not see is that his rent may vary in some manner with them. In fact, he feels impact and not incidence. What the landlord sees is that if he possesses two houses point to point the same, from the cellar damp to the attic wall-paper, offering like advantages, standing, maybe, side by side, but subject to different rates, then the rents will differ by the amount of the difference in rates. What he does not see is the general in the particular. In fact, he feels only a particular incidence.

In passing from the seen to the unseen it would be fruitful to go through the utterances of authority; but they are legion. Besides, paragraph summaries of systems of political economy have not proved strikingly successful. It is wiser, perhaps, for our purpose to be insular and brief. Yet in view of the prominence given to them, especially during the sittings of the Town Holdings Committee, it may be as well to mention in a few curt phrases, which only claim to indicate their main trend and not to express them, the violently opposed opinions of two distinguished thinkers. I am the more anxious to point to them as they lie at the opposite poles between which the orthodox economists take their stand, and as they serve to indicate the differences in doctrine which exist upon this subject.

Mr. Goschen says that the owner, *i.e.*, the landowner, pays the bulk, if not the whole, of the rates, unless their amount exceeds the average of those paid in the same locality prior to or at the time of the leasing of the site. When the average is exceeded, the excess falls on the house-owner or occupier, according to the state of demand and supply. Thorold Rogers maintained that the rates remained where first placed, that is, on the occupier. Professor Seligman has adopted and enforced the

same theory in his book on " The Shifting and
Incidence of Taxation."

Let us now turn from authority to the question itself.
It is necessary at the outset, in order to avoid the
confusions into which many have fallen, to define the
subject of our inquiry with some exactness. The
questions, Where do the rates fall? and, Who pays
the rates? are identical ; but they are not equivalent
to the question, What is the effect of the rates? It
is generally understood that the occupier pays the
whole or a part of the rates on the building which he
occupies, if the annual amount charged to him in rent
and rates exceeds the supply price of the house and
the economic rent of the land upon which it is built ;
that the house-owner pays the whole or a part of the
rates, if the net amount which he annually receives
falls below the supply price of the capital expended
on the building; and that the landowner contributes
exactly that amount by which his rent is less than it
would have been but for rates, on the supposition
that the quantity of land occupied and the manner of
its occupation remained as before. These are the
meanings which I believe are usually given to the
expression " the incidence of the rates." If we adopt
them, it is immediately obvious that the effect of the
rates is a larger question than that of the incidence of
the rates, for the former includes, besides the subject
matter of the narrower question, the reactions, following the imposition of rates, which raise or lower the

margin of building and affect the quantity and direction of capital. In the following discussion we shall be concerned primarily with the smaller question; but the wider one will be incidentally treated also.

The method here adopted is to ignore leases and other complications at first, and then to introduce them later as disturbing forces modifying the abstract results primarily reached. Let us begin the investigation by considering the case of houses.

In the long run the rate is divided between landowner and tenant; on the builder it cannot rest, for average profits and average self-interest protect him. But how is the division determined? The tax which falls on the house at "the margin" of building, that is, where there is no ground rent practically speaking, for instance on the twentieth storey of a Chicago "sky-scraper," falls on the occupier. But where there is ground rent a portion of the tax, in the ratio of real ground rent (whether paid or not) to the residue of rent, gets through to it ;[1] because building profits

[1] This is Mill's view (Bk. V. Ch. 3, § 6). It is really based on the assumption that the consumer does not estimate a site value in proportion to building value, but absolutely. For instance, it is supposed that, if there are two houses differing only in their situation whose rents are £40 and £80 respectively, the consumer considers the second to be worth, not twice as much as the former, whatever the rent of the former may be, but just £40 as much. Hence, if rates of fifty per cent. are imposed and he will pay a total (made up of rent and rates) of £60 for the former, his demand price (to include rates) for the

require that the tax on each unit of capital expended in building should be the same. Were it not so, capital, ever sensitive, would shun building.

We do not mean of course that the ground-rent holder is not affected at all. He is affected when supply price reacts on the quantity demanded. The view put forward is simply that the total sum paid by the occupier must equal (in the long run, of course) the normal cost of production of his accommodation and in addition the rates on it. Take for example a builder who has run up a house to nine storeys and is hesitating about the tenth. The tenth storey is then the marginal house. Assume that it will cost him an amount the expenditure of which is remunated by a rent of £30 a year. The rent must then tend to be £30. Let the rates on the £30 be £10. Now, who will pay them? Not the builder, for he would stop building at the ninth storey first. Not the landlord. Why should he? If these rates did force themselves on to him in any case, he would see to it that he let his land in future to a builder who would not go beyond the ninth storey, because the addition of a tenth would mean ten pounds out of his pocket. Then the occupier pays the ten pounds.

In brief, rates are divided between the occupier and

latter will be £100 and not £120. The question of how the estimate of the site value is determined cannot be said to be settled.

the ground-owner in the ratio of the value of the buildings to the value of the site.

Next observe the manner in which the ground-owner is touched. When rates go up the total paid by tenants for housing accommodation, *i.e.*, the sum of rents and rates, goes up also; but not by the amount of the increase in rates, only by the amount of the increase in those which fall on buildings. That being so, fewer houses will be wanted. Some who lived in palaces will move into mansions, some who occupied desirable messuages and tenements will find themselves satisfied with meaner edifices, and so forth down the scale of residences, till quite at the bottom there is a little more crowding than before. And this means that the *margin of building land has gone up;* and that consequently real ground-rents have fallen. But nevertheless the occupier still pays the rates at the new margin.

Again, the capitalist, as the landowner, may be prejudicially affected by the rates though he does not pay them. For capital may be driven from building, and there may be no fresh openings for investment, so that the increase of capital might be checked. Generally, however, the demand for capital will not diminish, since the expenditure of the income raised by rates frequently represents a demand for capital; and at most, therefore, there will be a redistribution of capital. The effect may simply be that more capital will be invested in streets and drains, and less in houses and other buildings. Of course, if the rates are expended in doing that, to render buildings habitable, which the builder previously did, the total of rent and rates cannot be raised to the occupier.

When a locality, all parts of which offer equal advantages, is divided between two rating authorities, the difference in rates drops on to the land—naturally, because rates have become *differential*, and rent is a payment for *differential advantages*.

The above is, in effect, the whole theory of the incidence of rates in the long period, with some discussion of their effects. Whether the objects of the rates be mansions or cottages, mills, warehouses, shops, farms, or railways, the theory is one. It is, nevertheless, desirable to show that the theory is one.

The tax on business premises and on plant is divided between consumer and landlord. In this case we have two sensitive capitals—that of the business occupier and that of the builder—except in so far as business premises have residential accommodation, which, by the forces described above, will impose on their occupiers the same taxes that they would pay if inhabiting houses proper with the same advantages. A part of the tax on shops may be shifted on to air; the builder will not pay that part, nor the landlord, nor the consumer, nor the occupier. The effect will be a decrease in shop accommodation. A fall in ground rents, and also a contraction of the conveniences offered to consumers when shopping, will accompany the killing of the old marginal shop.

The tax on railways (except the part paid by rail· way servants resident in buildings covered by the rateable value) is, of course, shared in the long run by the company *quâ* landlord and the consumer, except in so far as the railway is a monopoly.

The tax on agricultural land is divided between the consumer, the landlord, and the farmer ; the farmer paying as much as he would if he inhabited an equally desirable house in the district, and the landlord paying all rates on the value of the product due to the quality of the farm. The fundamental fact to be borne in mind is that rates vary with pro- duct, for they vary with rent, and rent varies with product. Hence the problem is really that of the tithe, which is treated by Mill in the third section of Chapter IV., Book V. of his Principles. Mill puts it in this way. After payment of the tithe :

" The land producing 100 bushels, reduced to 90, will yield a rent of 90-54, or 36 bushels.

" The land producing 90 bushels, reduced to 81, will yield a rent of 81-54, or 27 bushels.

" The land producing 80 bushels, reduced to 72, will yield a rent of 72-54, or 18 bushels.

" The land producing 70 bushels, reduced to 63, will yield a rent of 63-54, or 9 bushels."

The marginal land has been given as that producing
60 bushels, which, after payment of the tithe, had
only 54 bushels left for the farmer. Then Mill goes
on to argue that the price must rise, in the ratio of
the two marginal products, *i.e.*, 60/54; and that "the
landlords will therefore be compensated in value and
price for what they lose in quantity."

The discussion is quite correct, and valuable as far
as it goes. It is a little antiquated, or rather, wan-
tonly mediævalised, seeing that John Stuart Mill's
father introduced the method of "doses." To-day,
instead of only taking different lands producing so
many bushels, we should come a little nearer the
truth by considering the returns in bushels to different
"doses of labour and capital." Mill, again, neglects to
notice the rise in the *margin of cultivation* which
would follow the rise in the price of corn, and so
reduce rent and bring the price down somewhat.
The reader will be well aware that many difficulties
arise from the varying durabilities of the capital sunk
in the land, difficulties which must not be allowed to
absorb us here.

The outcome so far is as follows :—In the long
run payments for differential advantages—that is,
rents—tend to bear rates in proportion to the ratio of
economic rent to gross rent; and it must be remembered that the quantity of rates determines to some
extent the different advantages of different localities.
The remainder of the rates, which is not "rolled

on to air," is borne by residential occupiers and by consumers.

The next step in the argument should naturally be the introduction of modifications resulting from leases and the social friction which prevents rapid repercussion from bringing ultimate incidence close in time to impact, and which causes it, moreover, to be influenced by impact. I have decided, however, to leave impact to the end of the chapter. It is really no use discussing it until the equities, or otherwise, of incidence have been settled. The latter is then our present objective.

How should society distribute the cost of local operations?

The reader need not be under any alarm. There is no intention of introducing here, as a digression, a treatise on the principles of taxation, though such a treatise would be by no means irrelevant. Most principles will be assumed, and their outcome will be only roughly indicated.

The following proposition is fundamental and indisputable. When the benefit resulting from optional works can be traced, their cost at least should be fixed on the recipients;[1] and when it cannot, the cost

[1] This is not quite true, since there are cases in which benefit can be localised, but in which it is desirable for the community as a whole that the consumer should employ the service more than he would if he paid the cost of his use of it. In such cases payment is best made on the basis of ability, or on that of some recognised standards of the quantity of service the members of

should be borne by the units of the local body politic in proportion to their ability to pay, as should also the cost of all compulsory services which remains to the locality.

There are, generally speaking, three classes of people paying rates, if the preceding analysis of the incidence of rates is correct:

1. Residential occupants.
2. Consumers.
3. Ground-rent owners.

The shares, if any, which ought to be paid by each, must now be determined.

1. *Residential occupants* should be taxed for their share, which we shall see later is residual, according to their ability to pay, as they are units of the local body politic. Ability is now measured by the rent of the home. Is this rent a satisfactory test? Let us examine a few objections.

Sismondi, among his maxims of taxation, has two of great importance. They are:

(1) Taxation should never touch what is necessary for the existence of the contributor.

(2) Taxation should not put to flight the wealth on which it is imposed.

A tax in space, it is urged, especially on houses, offends against both of these maxims. Shelter, light, and pure air, are necessary for bare existence ; a

each class ought to employ. Water may be taken as an example.

certain amount of privacy is necessary for healthy social life. High rates breed congestion. The case is not yet fully stated. To pass from the depths to respectable middle-class quarters, even here the house is said to be no very accurate of ability. Professor Seligman believes that it is the best test, and his opinion must carry great weight. We agree at once as regards rents above a certain amount and below a certain amount, but under the lower limit the size of the house simply indicates the size of the family. In partial rejoinder, it may be urged that the very same objection applies to almost all taxes.

The indictment has another count. A house of a certain size is practically all that is wanted, whether the income be twenty thousand pounds or forty thousand pounds. There is point in the contention. It is very largely true that after the income passes some limit the size of the house varies in a less ratio than the income. Nevertheless, the conclusions intended are to some extent, but not entirely, weakened by the fact that more than one establishment will be supported from the largest incomes.

None of the above arguments[1] prove that the rates are essentially vitiated as taxes according to

[1] There is another, which has been previously indicated, that perhaps the occupier only pays rates varying with the building rent of his house, whereas his ability more likely varies as the gross rent. Probably, as usual, the truth as to the incidence of rates lies in the mean, and the occupier does pay some portion at any rate of the share which Mill held to fall on the ground

ability. The objections pointed to are common to most imposts. Moreover, in the case of rates, there is a possible reform by which most of them could be obviated. That reform is the grading of rates. The grading of rates does exist now in a very small degree in the slight benefit accruing to the tenant when the landlord pays the rates and receives some remission for doing so. But it has been estimated that, as at present constituted, rates are "regressive," that is, they bear more heavily on the poor than on those in easy circumstances. We have an excellent example of "degression" (that is, less than proportional progression) in the imperial tax based on the occupation of houses. [1]

owner. However that may be, it is quite certain that the localities have no other test of ability than that afforded by rent, or a portion of it, and practically even the portion, I am inclined to think, provides about as good a criterion of ability as any which the local or central government can lay its hand upon.

[1] INHABITED HOUSE DUTIES.

On shops, beerhouses, farmhouses and lodging-houses of an annual value,

Less than £20	. nil in the £
Of £20 but not exceeding £40	. 2d. „ „ „
Exceeding £40 but not exceeding £60 .	. 4d. „ „ „
„ £60 „ „ „ .	. 6d. „ „ „

On dwelling-houses of an annual value,

Less than £20	. nil in the £
Of £20 but not exceeding £40 . . .	. 3d. „ „ „
Exceeding £40 but not exceeding £60 .	. 6d. „ „ „
„ £60 „ „ „ .	. 9d. „ „ „

Partially business residences are moreover charged
by this tax at a lower rate. Few objections of any
weight can be found to the adoption of some like
system with respect to rates. Against increasing the
rate per pound for high rents little can be said; and
much can be said in its favour. A portion of such a
rate becomes a tax on social distinction, and such a
tax, as the Duke of Devonshire has pointed out,
blesses, or at any rate satisfies, both him that gives
and him that receives.

The grading of rates is desirable, provided certain
cautions are observed. Some arise from the facts of
the shifting of rates. These we had better examine at
once. Imagine the rate in the £ steadily increasing with the rent. Where and how would the increased rates fall? The answer depends upon the
variants underlying differences in rents. They are two.
Firstly, variations in the value of the site, secondly,
variations in the value of the buildings. Now, in so
far as the variations in gross rents are due to the
former cause, the degressive part of the rate will tend
to fall on the ground owner; but, in the degree in
which they are due to the size and quality of the
building, the degressive burden will tend to come on
to the occupiers. The conclusion follows directly
from the foregoing theory of the incidence of rates.
If the rate varied not as the rent but as the quality of
the building, say as the number of rooms or something of that kind (compare for instance the hearth

tax and window tax) its degression would find out
the occupier and refuse to pass on to the ground-rent
holder.

The above considerations give rise to the question,
What is required? Is it desirable to cut off a slice of
ground-values in tempering taxation to the struggling
lower middle-class? My own opinion is, that, in
view of existing conditions and expectations, legislation with the dual object would be objectionable.
The time has come to deal with ground-values; and
to be dealt with scientifically they must clearly be
trèated apart on the basis of a separate valuation.
It is confusing to have two or three legislative
measures, when one is sufficient, and in the resulting complications inequities can easily hide themselves. Besides it is prudent to avoid, at all moderate
costs, adding fuel to the still merrily blazing debate
on the incidence of taxes. When the actual facts
about the bearing of burdens become matter for controversy we may be sure that the truth is being
obscured by *ex parte* arguments, and that injustices are
being perpetrated and perpetuated. The rates which
are intended to be borne by occupiers should be
treated apart, and graded to meet differences in
abilities to pay.

One other caution with reference to all reform in
taxation. If any rate which comes down on the land
anywhere is eased, a free gift is made to many
holders of ground rents, for by amortisation early

burdens remain with the owners at the time of imposition. If the land has changed hands the new holder really pays no part of them, as taxes were in effect capitalised and taken off the purchase money.

2. *The consumer's share of rates.* The rates on business premises which do not rest in the land are passed over to the consumers. By what right are consumers called upon to pay this share?—people who are not units in the local body politic, who may be living miles away from the locality, even in other countries. By what right does Bolton tax the Babu on his native soil? By the right to demand full value for value received. These rates are justified so far only as they represent part of the cost of production of commodities. The local government paves the streets, and lights them, and cleans them, and preserves order, for instance; and the cost of these operations is evidently part of the cost of production of the commodities manufactured, or transported, traded in, or in some manner operated upon, in the spot referred to.

The whole of the rates on the business premises which escape the land are here regarded as passing over to the consumer. Strictly speaking this view is not correct. Certain portions, standing for the differential personal comforts of producers, remain upon them. They are to be regarded as half-day resident occupiers, and as such they should contribute

according to ability to the cost of that portion of
local works which is not attributable to the wear and
tear of business *qua* business. As regards the surplus
local operations, each business should subscribe to
their cost according to the proportion of them which
it exhausts. What they shall be the majority must
determine. If it decides upon wood-paving, then no
business has the right to say, "We will pay the
hypothetical cost of the wear and tear by our cart
of granite sets, which are all that we require." If
such a business cannot bear the cost of its destruction
of wooden sets, it must go elsewhere.

The question of the best practical method of
coming near the equitable in the abstract is one of
the utmost difficulty. It is a question which requires
an intimate knowledge of practical details. That
under the existing arrangements the approximation
is only very rough, and, further, that special businesses are greatly over-weighted, is certain. Take
railways for instance. It is proved up to the hilt
that railway companies are over-rated, that they are
fleeced more than is justified by the benefits they
derive from the services of local authorities; that, in
a word, they are heavily taxed instead of being
charged the market price for an element in the cost
of carriage. It may be counter-claimed that the
rates on railways are a device for taxing the whole
country in aid of the localities. Then it is a very
foolish device, because cheap transportion is so

valuable a boon that no impediments should be cast
in its way.

Take the following picked figures, showing the
rateable value of the Great Western Railway and
that of certain parishes through which it passes.

	Rateable value of G.W.R.	Total rateable value of Parish.
Newport	£5,724	£7,483
St. Devereux	4,114	5,225
Baulking	4,045	6,060
Grove (Berks)	6,240	9,225

It is obviously absurd that the railway company
should continue to play the part of a fairy god-
mother. The plea put forward by the rating agent
to the Great Western Railway that the system of
differential rating for land and railways as authorised
under the Public Health Act, 1875, be extended to
several other rates, seems modest in the extreme.[1]

The whole system of rating business premises,
machinery, and so forth, requires the careful revision
of specialists. But any revision will be worthless
unless it is definitely recognised that the basis of the
contribution of businesses, *qua* businesses, to the cost
of local operations is the quantity of exhaustion of
the local services in production. Of course, only the
roughest approximation to abstract justice is possible.[2]

[1] "Commission on Local Taxation," Vol. I. Part II., p. 368.

[2] When it is stated that businesses ought to contribute to the
cost of local operations in proportion to the quantity of the

3. *Ground-rent owners.* The owners of real ground-rent are meant, not only those who receive part, or all, or more than all, of the annual ground value under contract. The demand for contributions from them for the conduct of local work is founded on the production of much of the value which they hold by the activities of local bodies.

Does the ground-rent bear now more than a just share according to the above test? Clearly not, for though conditions are such that we cannot say how much of the increased value of sites is due, directly and indirectly, to what the locality does, and how much to the growth of population and the great sum of unmeasurable and undefinable causes which govern the segregation of human beings, yet it is certain that the small fraction of augmented value which is substracted from the ground value through the medium of rates does not cover the wealth which is given to the ground-owners directly by the paving of streets, lighting, policing, sanitation, and the many other services performed by local popular governments.

We find many suggestions and much agitation for

outcome of those operations which they exhaust, the question may be asked, "But why, then, should not indirect imperial taxes be regulated in the same way?" One answer is, because they are taxes and not merely remunerations for services. The nation may tax home consumers as constituents of the State, but Manchester may not tax a resident in London because he is not a constituent of Manchester.

carrying the principle of payment for value received into effect.

There is firstly " betterment," a proposal which is put forward as specially important in view of the fact that the increase in urban rates is largely caused by optional works, most of which have a market value. A select committee of the House of Lords, appointed in 1894 to consider the proposal, defined " betterment " as " the principle that persons whose property has clearly been increased in market value by an improvement effected by local authorities should specially contribute to the cost of the improvement." In other words, payment must be in proportion to benefit whenever benefit can be definitely tracked down. To raise the cry of compensation for " worsement " is to confuse issues. The principle of " worsement " is applied to-day to actual positive damage, and only so far is it justifiable. Claims for compensation can scarcely be based on an alteration in the ratio of advantages of two situations caused by the improvement of the one, the other remaining as before ; but it is unfair that the owner of the former should gain and pay no more than he does in the increased rates which come with increased value. As it is to-day in the United Kingdom for the actual, positive, and specific betterment, the local community as a whole pays, not excluding even the persons whose interests are prejudiced by the improvements. If the services were competitively performed, the market price of the work done would be paid by the benefited parties, and it should be paid by them also (or, at any rate, some part of it) if the work is undertaken by the local executive.

Another suggested remedy for the leakage of social wealth is the taxation of ground-rents. Society in its dealings with urban land-owners is finding itself much in the position of Laban in his last transaction with Jacob. All its cattle are somehow getting the specks and spots and ring strakes which mark them as the property of the ground-owner. It is proposed to tax ground-rents even when the cause of the increased value cannot be directly traced to local works. It may be adversely reasoned that the ground-owner, in the case of a long lease, receives an unvarying sum each year, and that therefore, as his income does not increase, he must not be specially taxed. This argument overlooks the fact that, although the actual income may be as before, the capital value may have increased greatly through increased value in the property which secures it. It is part of this increased value which the reform would assure to the community. Against all taxation of future values the general argument is used that in purchase they have been taken into consideration. What force there is in the suggestion is diminished by the facts that only a portion of the increased value would be confiscated, and that risks also have been taken into account in estimates of future values.

Neither of the above proposed reforms necessitates that general valuation of sites, which has been regarded in the past as impracticable. But as the valuation of sites is being made every day it is ceasing to be so regarded. I am inclined to regard the taxation of contract ground-rents as one-sided (in view of the wider basis afforded by the valuation of sites), in that it overlooks the ground-value held by the lessee. It is plain that the rates should come down, on the whole ground-value, and not only on the one portion brought within reach by the accidents of contract.

But the question of the taxation of ground-values is best treated, for reasons which will appear later, after a discussion of the relation of impact to incidence.

Impact and Incidence.—Seeing that this chapter has already proceeded to wearisome length, and moreover that the modifications which actuality imposes on our conclusions as to incidence may be left without danger to the reader to apply for himself, I do not intend to say much upon the question.

The impact of taxes is of great importance for two reasons.

(1) Social friction prevents the easy and rapid rolling of taxes.

(2) Legal contracts, in the form of leases, may prevent the incidence described above.

Such facts give the colour of truth to Mr. Blunden's statement [1] that all increases of rates in congested, and exceptionally advantageous, and decaying districts, are paid by the landlord of the buildings; for in the former two cases he is able to exact a monopoly rent, and in the latter case, high rates or low rates, there are empty houses all around.

The occupier with a lease whether of a farm, business premises, or residential property, of course pays increase of rates. The farmer and other producers cannot immediately shift the increase on to the consumers by reducing their output, and the landlord is secured by the lease. And the occupier without a lease—we must almost say, "of course he pays increase of rates," for there is a social friction which checks the rolling of taxes, and the cost and trouble of removing, and the loss therein involved, so far as business premises are concerned, by reason of the good-will resulting from the habits of customers, and, so far as houses are concerned, by reason of the *pretium affectionis*, the drag of old associations, are facts to be reckoned with. It is in view of all this, and of the fact that first incidence does affect final incidence, that Mr. Goschen, and other influential writers and statesmen, urged the division of rates in the first incidence between occupier, house-owner, and ground-owner, the last two sharing half the rates in proportion to the rents received by each. This principle was intro-

[1] "Local Taxation and Finance," p. 55.

duced by Mr. Goschen into a bill, brought forward in
1871, which, however, was subsequently suffered to
drop. Systems of division of rates between occupiers
and land-owners have been in operation in both Scotland and Ireland for many years past. The principle
is excellent, provided that the separate valuation of
ground-values is impracticable. But if it is not, something much nearer perfection is open to us.

Let us here, for the sake of clearness, pause for one
moment to recapitulate and summarise. The fundamental basis upon which the conclusions put forward
in this chapter stand are as follows :—

It is required to tax occupiers, ground-rent holders,
and consumers. The tax on each of them is of an
absolutely different character, and the variations in
each should, therefore, be governed entirely by considerations in its own domain. There is no reason
in the world why the occupier's ability to pay, or the
cost of productive processes undertaken by the locality,
should vary as the value given to the land by the operations of the sectional government. It is therefore
absurd to think to obtain the three ends above set
forth by a single tax on one class of people (occupiers)[1]
on a common basis (rent). Even if we were justifiably
optimistic—which we simply cannot be—as to the immediate following of incidence in impact, it would still
be absurd.

[1] The present system results in an absurd restriction of the
franchise in the modern city-state.

This is the only one scientific method of procedure, if the above basis of local taxation is accepted.

To value sites apart from buildings.

Then to tax :—

Sites according to the value given to them.

Residential occupiers according to their ability.

Business occupiers [1] according to the cost of the services by which their businesses are assisted. But the proportion of rateable value to be taxed in the cases of particular businesses, and the question of allowances and so forth, should be settled by the central government to secure uniformity.

To act on these suggestions we have been told is quite beyond the scope of practical politics, because a separate valuation of the site cannot be obtained. Conclusive evidence is, however, wanting in support of the contention. Mr. Fletcher Moulton in the debate in the Queen's speech, on Feb. 10th, 1899, said, " It was amusing to see the way in which people dropped their hands and said, ' It is impossible ; you cannot separate the values.' He challenged the Attorney General with his unrivalled experience in compensation cases under the Lands Clauses Act to deny his statement that whenever they made the surveyors value the house and land, the first thing they did was

---

[1] Business men, *qua* half-residents in the business centre, ought to contribute something additional also ; but there is no reason why those who do not happen to be tenants should be exempt from local taxes.

to value the land separately, and then they considered what the house added to it. In fact, the attempt to make it difficult to value accurately and relatively the value of the land site as distinguished from the value of the house was perfectly hopeless." His assertion was not denied. Moreover, a list of valuation of sites has been prepared for London. It was handed into the present commission by Mr. G. L. Gomme. It is asserted that such lists can be drawn up without much difficulty ; that they are in fact always being drawn up by valuers, though not separately published. The fear of sinister influences operating in their preparation is little greater than in the case of existing lists of rateable values. We may take it that the separate valuation of sites is not impracticable.

The impact of the tax intended to abide with the occupier must, of course, be in the occupier. The impact of the tax intended to be rolled on to the consumers must, of course, be on the occupier, because he is closer to the ultimate bearers than the landlord. And the impact of the tax intended to fall on the ground-value must be—where ? Some of the ground-rent is an unvarying sum fixed by contract to be paid annually to some person or persons. The remainder, a variable, is received by the lessee of the plot, in part only perhaps, part being received by the lessee of the building. The best way, then, of getting at the ground-value, is to impose the whole of the tax on the owner of the building, and to empower him to deduct the proportional parts of the amount of the tax from each contractual rent which he pays. This method is much simpler than seeking out the owners of the contractual rents and imposing their share on them direct. An obvious objection, however, is that the owner of the building may have to pay a tax on a portion of the ground-value received by the occupier under lease. For the sake of simplicity this defect, which is not likely to be great, is best left to the correction of economic forces. It is moreover obvious that it is more the function of the property speculator than of the occupier to shoulder these short-period risks. It may be easy to value a site and so get at the economic rent, but in the case of agricultural land it is so difficult as to be almost impracticable, since capital, both long enduring and rapidly exhaustive, is mixed up with it. To insure the share which falls ultimately on the land, and which is large, not getting shifted for short periods somewhere else, there is much to be said for allowing the farmer to deduct rates from his rent, the house being treated separately as other residences.

From the foregoing discussion it is apparent, and the next chapter will render it still more apparent, that the bitterest complaints as to the burden and inequities of the rates are founded, so far as they have foundation, not on any essential defects in the system of rates, but on existing accidental and removable arrangements. Local taxation, if reformed on the abstract lines above laid down to the extent to which it is practicable, would show no great inferiority, in equity and economy, to imperial taxation. But to attempt to remove existing blots by means of subventions is to adopt the most indirect and the least plausible method of repairing defects, and then, far from repairing, to aggravate them.

CHAPTER VI

DIFFERENTIAL RATES AND THEIR CAUSES

THE quantitative dissimilarities in rates in different localities now claim some consideration. For a successful examination the mind must be kept constantly alive to the fact that the question proposed at each stage is of a composite nature. It is really twofold, with one of its alternatives three-headed ; thus,

(1) Do any of the differences in rates, or in any part of them, necessitate some measure of equalisation ?

(2) If so, is the necessity met most satisfactorily by (*a*) extending boundaries, *i.e.*, by giving legal sanction to the conception that the local organism is bigger than its present paper description, (*b*) county assistance, or (*c*) State assistance.

The remark will not be out of place here, as a word of tacit warning, that almost without exception the second head of the complex alternative, and the first head also, we might add, have been entirely overlooked by those who have been most importunate in their demands for the relief of rates. It has been pretty nearly universally assumed that the sole choice lies between the *status quo* and imperial largess.

Here is a quotation from a table constructed by Mr. Cannan, in which the rates, and expenditure on different objects, of all the county boroughs in England and Wales are shown.

(From Mr. Cannan's Article in " Economic Journal," Vol. V., p. 27.)

RATES IN SOME ENGLISH COUNTY BOROUGHS, AND
EXPENDITURE ON DIFFERENT OBJECTS IN 1890-91.

County Borough.	Rateable Value per head.	Pence in £ expended on				Total Rate Raised.	Rate per Head of Population.
		Sewage.	Streets.	Police.	Schools.		
	£	D.	D.	D.	D.	D.	£ s. D.
Norwich	2·55	9	19	10	20	82	0 17 7
Preston	3·87	4	10	7	0	57	0 14 10
Southampton	2·76	1	6	7	8	53	0 16 7
Halifax	3·86	4	11	6	20	51	0 16 4
Gateshead ...	2·81	1	6	7	11	47	0 11 0
Wigan	2·57	25	15	10	1	47	0 10 1
Hastings	6·76	2	12	3	3	44	1 4 11
Manchester..	5·47	2	9	9	4	43	0 19 11
Liverpool....	5·79	3	1	11	4	38	0 18 7
Bath	5·34	2	14	6	1	37	0 16 8
St. Helens...	3·67	0	7	6	0	33	0 10 2
Oldham......	4·42	8	7	5	4	28	0 10 3

It will be seen that the total rates vary from 7s. in Norwich to 2s. 4d. in Oldham. Like varieties are to be found among urban districts. This difference in rates is *prima facie* hardly consistent with justice, but further analysis may lead us to modify our judgment. Let us begin by separating the cost of the material works from that of the personal works of local bodies. By "material works" is meant operations directly on things, by "personal works" those directly on persons. The distinction is adopted merely to provide classes suitable for easy manipulation. It is not the same as that between "optional" and "necessary," or between "beneficial" and "onerous" works.

If we confine our attention solely to the material functions of boroughs we still find enormous differences in rates. The amount expended on sewage in Wigan, for instance, came to 3s. 4d. in the £, whereas in Southampton, Gateshead, and St. Helens, it was only 7d. in the £, and in Liverpool only 4d. The following examples of the general district rates of boroughs other than county boroughs for 1895-6 further illustrate this quantitative unlikeness :—

Bacup, 2s. 4d.   Bedford, 3s.   Bradford, 1s. 10d.
Hyde, 3s. 6d.   Wigan, 4s. 6d.   Wakefield, 4s.
Godalming, 5s. 2d.

The causes of differences may be tabulated as follows :—[1]

[1] With respect to much of the following discussion I am

I. In some places the rateable value per head is greater than in others.[1]

II. In some places the works cost more than in others on account of geographical, topographical, and other circumstances over which the local bodies have no control. This is of special importance in the case of sewage works.

III. In some places the cost is greater than in others owing to inefficient management.

IV. Some places have larger returns to capital invested in the past, some are investing more capital in the present.

V. Some places have a larger income besides that from rates, for instance, from unpurchased endowments.

VI. The local works of some places are of greater variety than those of others, and superior in kind.

VII. Some places have more contracted boundaries than others.[2]

largely indebted to Mr. Cannan's article on " Inequality of Local Rates and its Economic Justification " in Vol. V. of the *Economic Journal.*

[1] One cause of this is the proportion of property wholly or partially exempted from rates within the district.

[2] In heterogeneous districts, that is those partly residential and partly given over to business, there is another reason for differences in rates, in addition to the seven causes above enumerated. This eighth cause, which applies also to personal services, but which will now be treated once and for all in this note, is the proportion of the rateable value of business premises to that of residential premises. If businesses are over-taxed by the rates, that is, if they pay more than the cost of their wear

These causes will now be examined seriatim with a view to determining whether they offer any reason for assistance from the imperial exchequer.

I. There is no more reason for other bodies to bear part of the cost of local material works, which are entirely optional, of poor districts, than to pay part of the cost of the poor man's living. Each is on the same plane, since outside interest in these works is inappreciable compared with local interests. The claim for assistance to poor districts on the ground of the cost of their optional works involves the whole ethical and economic question of the distribution of wealth which is without the bounds of this essay. But, in so far as the operations are compulsory, sanitary works, for instance, low rateable value[1] is ground for relief, and it has been recognised as such by the Equalisation of Rates Act, which will be referred to later. Measures of such a character as that Act seem to meet the hardship adequately and with

and tear and general exhaustion of local works, then the greater the proportion of business premises to houses the less have residential occupants to contribute to the cost of local functions. The sole method of removing this ground of injustice is to carefully determine the relative amounts which businesses *qua* businesses ought to contribute to the local funds. In all probability an investigation with this object in view would result in the rejection, to a great extent at any rate, of rent as a basis for taxation.

[1] It will be pointed out later that existing rateable values are unreliable on account of different degrees of under-valuation and of a variety of systems. The official rateable value cannot therefore be taken as a correct measure of relative wealth.

fewer drawbacks than exchequer contributions, the former being founded, as the latter are not, on the result of scientific analysis.

II. Geographical and topographical disadvantages are frequently offset by advantages in the locality, for instance, climate, harbours, waterway, coal, and so forth. The calculation of natural utilities and disutilities is practically impossible, and if it were not, no more claim could be based upon a balance of loss than upon the mistakes made by any individual in choosing a trade by which his income is rendered less than it might have been.

III. No words are needed under this head. Efficiency is the business of the locality.

IV. Few words are needed under this head. The investment of capital is a matter of management which must rest with the locality. On the one hand works may be costly and enduring, on the other cheap and ephemeral. Capital may be borrowed and invested at once, or investment may be delayed. These are questions of economy to be duly weighed by local bodies.

V. I have no ground of complaint if A. presents an income to B. and I am neglected, and it matters not whether B. be a person or a locality. When the gifts to localities are of great age, the central government has some reason for interference on the ground that the present beneficiary is not the same as the one to which the gift was made, or that the benefit has undesirable results ; but care must be exercised that the generosity of the subject to the locality be not checked.

VI. No assistance can be grounded here. If my living costs more than A.'s, because it is more luxurious, am I therefore to be compensated? Some towns have roads of wood and of concrete, promenades and fountains, parks, statues, and art galleries ; and for these they must pay.

So much for the first six causes of the differences in rates with regard to the material functions of localities. We find in them no claim for subventions from the imperial exchequer. Nor do they convey any reason for assistance from any treasuries at a distance, with one exception, sanitation. The seventh cause, however, the extent of the locality, reveals an exasperating grievance, that those living outside the administrative area of some local body, but at no considerable distance, share the benefits of the local works without sharing in the cost. For example, the consumer in the suburbs who makes his purchases in the towns and takes much of his re-creation there ; the manufacturer just outside the city boundary who shares almost all the local business benefits to the cost of which he pays nothing ; those just over the border of the county borough of Manchester, to whose prosperity the Ship Canal contributes, but who escape the Ship Canal rate ; the farmers round the market town whose carts plough up the town streets at no cost to themselves.

It may be taken as sufficiently true for our purpose that the heaviest expenditure lies about the centre of the town. Hence at the boundaries ratepayers are contributing more than is laid out in their immediate locality. The rates of a town will fall as a rule if its boundaries are extended ; but if the town opens out, local self-government must apparently be withdrawn from urban districts. Hence a very disturbing dilemma. The best solution is to refuse both alternatives. The explanation of the seeming paradox is simple. It cannot be said exactly at what age a lamb becomes a sheep, neither can the spot be indicated at which the town as an organic whole ends. Is it not possible in some degree to carry the skirts of the one district over contiguous districts, when the former happens to possess, as a town always does, a wide sweep of outer area, which is nevertheless to a great extent one with the centre? [1]

It has been suggested that zones of rateable area might be instituted round urban centres; these zones to be chargeable, with respect to certain works, at rates diminishing with distance from the centre. By this means the burden of town rates would be somewhat diminished. Some such reform is becoming

[1] In the adjustment of financial relations between counties and county boroughs the services performed by the former for the latter were taken into consideration by the Commissioners.

more urgent every day as the movement to the suburbs, not only for residence but also for manufacture, gains force, largely through cheapened means of transit and transport. Of course, it cannot be laid down in this brief sketch that the adoption of rateable zones [1] is the reform needed. All that we can assert is that it is the kind of reform needed. A better project, perhaps, is that districts should be grouped like parishes in unions, and that a governing body should be set over the group for the management of those affairs which were the intimate concern of larger organisms than the districts; for instance, a city and its surrounding urban districts are one for many purposes and their government should mark this partial oneness. It would be a great relief to get the urban organisms out of their straight waistcoats.

We have now to consider the difference in rates due to the personal functions of localities. They are

[1] It is worthy of notice that we have to-day in operation in some places a system practically cognate to that of rateable zones. Some cities, for instance, which manufacture their own gas and which supply it to surrounding urban districts, charge for it more than the market price. To take an example; the Gas Committee at Manchester has this year handed over £52,000, gained on their working, to the City Fund. The dangers which may easily arise from abuses of this system are evident. Besides, the system does not ensure that all districts will be treated alike. Stretford, for instance, one of the districts round Manchester, does not receive its gas from the city supplies. A big tax, again, may easily be collected with the water rate.

the preservation of order and security, the maintenance of the poor, and education. In the case of
county boroughs, in 1890-91, the cost of the police
varied from 11d. in the £ at Liverpool to 3d. in the
£ at Hastings; the cost of education from 1s. 8d. in
the £ at Norwich and Halifax to nothing at Preston
and in many other towns.[1] To give another example,
the police in 1890-91 cost 4'7d. in the £ (calculated
in the Metropolitan Poor Rate valuation) in London,
and 2d. in the £ in the counties. Again, in 1890-91
the school board rate in London was 9'7d. in the £,
but in the boroughs only 5'1d. Take the poor
rate again. In 1893 it was 17'8d in the £ in
London and 10'8d. for all extra-metropolitan districts.
The difference in the poor rates in some of the
parishes in England and Wales in 1891 are given
below.

Poor Rates, excluding precept rates, in some Unions and
Parishes under separate Boards of Guardians in 1891 (from
Fowler's " Report on Local Taxation ") :—

	S.	D.		S.	D.
City of London .	1	0'4	St. George in the East	0	10'3
Woolwich. . .	2	3'7	Reigate . . .	0	5'2
Southampton .	1	5'0	Great Yarmouth. .	1	11'0
Nottingham .	0	11'9	Tarvin . . .	0	1'5
Altrincham . .	0	1'2	Manchester . .	0	7'9
Liverpool . .	0	6'8	Monmouth . . .	2	0'3
Cardiff . _ .	0	10'0	Carnarvon . . .	2	8'5
Conway . .	0	8'6			

[1] See Table, p. 67.

The following table from the Local Taxation Returns shows the poor rates in each of the eleven divisions of English and Welsh Unions in 1894-5 :—

	£	s.	d.			£	s.	d.
Metropolitan .	o	3	2	West Midland .	o	2	1¼
South-West .	o	2	3	North . . .	o	1	9¼
East . .	o	2	9¼	North-West . .	o	1	11¾
South-East .	o	2	2¾	York . . .	o	2	3¾
South Midland	o	2	2¼	North . . .	o	1	7½
Welsh . .	o	2	6¾				

Enough evidence has been given to prove that the differences in rates arising from the cost of the personal functions of localities are great—sufficiently great to induce an examination into expenditure under the three heads.

Education.—The variations in the cost per £ of education are due to (*a*) voluntary effort; (*b*) differences in rateable value per head of districts ; and (*c*) the quality of the educational work done and the efficiency of school boards.

As regards the first cause no objection can be made. The endowed schools exist, and if they do their work well,- and are centrally and popularly controlled, the need for board schools is less. No importance can be attached to the complaint that the distribution of endowed schools throughout the country is not sporadic. It is one case of gifts which have already been considered.

The local community may more justly have a helping hand extended to it on the plea of a low rateable value per head. It is understood by the principle of free education that the cost of education must be distributed proportionally to ability. The test of ability should theoretically be extended to the division of the cost between the locality and the imperial treasury. If we assume that the division of interest in education between the nation as a whole and the locality is practically the same in all cases, then the money measure of this interest will vary with the wealth of the locality, because of the diminishing utility of money. If the contention be admitted, then the amount of the Government grants should vary inversely with the rateable value per head of the district—the true rateable value. The Government does to some extent recognise its responsibility to poor districts by making special grants, which are accorded in cases in which the actual expenses of a school board during any year amount to a sum which would have been raised by a rate of 3d. in the £ on the rateable value of the district, and when any such rate would have produced less than £20, or less than 7s. 6d. per child of the number of children in average attendance during the year at the schools provided by the school boards. Again, that the Government does not feel that too much of the cost of education is being discharged by it, is demonstrated by the fact that the additional subventions made over to Scotland were applied to the relief of school fees.

The solution above suggested is not quite sound, because it ignores the responsibilities of the near localities. Moreover, it suffers from complexities. An alternative which at once insinuates itself is the extension of the school district. It is generally admitted that the parish is too minute a unit for educational purposes, and that even the districts formed by most of the existing unions of parishes are too small. By the widening of school districts more efficient management would be secured, because members of the school board would be drawn from a larger field, which would offer of course a more varied selection of candidates, and a higher grade of ability would be attracted because of the increased dignity of office and the greater responsibility attendant on further-reaching control. There is no special reason in the case of education, as in poor relief, for small administrative districts. The expansion of the district within limits can bring with it nothing but gain. It goes without saying that there would be greater uniformity in the rateable value per head in larger districts.

The differences in school rates resulting from differences in the quality of educational work done introduces a difficult question. The Government requires a certain standard : anything above that may be viewed as a work of supererogation, and as dangerous, because it may add another fold to the overlapping of the regions of operation of different educational organs. We have an example in the existing competition between secondary board schools, lavishly equipped, and many grammar schools, too scantily supported by their towns—a competition through which the grammar school is rendered less capable of doing the higher work demanded of it (which the secondary board school cannot do), and through which, therefore, the children are made to suffer. Still, if overlapping could be prevented, it would be well for a central authority to vary its grant somewhat with the quality of the work done.

Police.—The differences in expenses are principally due to rateable value and the special requirements of some towns arising from some disorderly elements in their population. Mr. Cannan's table [1] shows that among county boroughs there are 21 cases in which high rateable value per head is accompanied by low police expenditure, and only five cases in which high value and high police expenditure, or low value and low police expenditure, go together. The four towns which have high rateable value and high police expenditure are Liverpool, Newcastle, Bristol, and Manchester. The reason, of course, is the exceptional roughness of a part of their population. The first two of the towns are flourishing seaports, the third has still much shipping, and the fourth is but a

[1] *Economic Journal,* Vol. V., p. 27.

day's tramp from Liverpool, and has, moreover, a miniature port of its own. The requirements of the Home Office being such that considerable uniformity in expenditure per head of population is secured, offers a partial explanation of the inverse variations above referred to.

The contention with respect to education that the Government grant should vary inversely with rateable value per head of the district, might be urged with equal force here. And so might the same objection. It is a question for the practical politician to decide whether the gain in justice is worth the loss in simplicity and uniformity. The work of policing a town is of such nature, and is so regulated, that no inefficiency or waste is likely to result from increased subsidies. Mr. W. A. Hunter,[1] indeed, enters a vehement protest against any such conclusion, and points in support of his contention to the fact that the expenses of police have risen in Scotland with subventions from $8\frac{1}{2}$d. in 1854 to 1s. 10d. in 1893. The facts must be admitted, but the causal nexus may be denied. Mr. W. H. Smith has pointed out in the *Economic Journal*[2] that the rise may be accounted for thus:—"(1) The rising wages of the class whence the police are drawn ; (2) that on paper a new body always appears cheaper than it really is, for at first all salaries are at a minimum, and pro-

[1] " Lecture on Local and Imperial Taxation," 1894.
[2] Vol. V., p. 184.

vision for pensions, etc., is not thought of—these de-
ferred charges must be added to the expenditure of
the earlier years to get a true figure for comparison;
and (3) that the officers in question from time to time
have had imposed upon them 'police' duties which
are altogether outside their sphere of service as mere
constables."

Poor Relief.—The causes of the enormous diver-
gences in the amounts of poor rate are—(*a*) differences
in rateable value per head, (*b*) differences in the numbers of paupers, and (*c*) differences in economy of
management.

The third cause may be set aside at once; in it
there is no ground for relief.

The differences under the first head are very
great. To take a few selected examples in England
in 1891-2; the rateable value per head in Eaststone-
house was £2 12s.; in the City of London, £107;
in Wallsall, £2 13s; and in Bellingham, £14 8s.
The first two cases are, however, exceptional. Mr.
Cannan points out [1] that of the 195 unions which
have an expenditure per head under 5s., 100 have a
value per head of less than £4 18s., and only 52 have
a value of more than £6 6s.; while of the 208 unions
which have an expenditure of more than 7s., 45 have
a value under £4 18s., and no less than 73 have a
value over £6 6s. On the ground of these differences
relief from the Treasury may legitimately be claimed

[1] *Economic Journal*, Vol. V., p. 25.

—that is, a relief varying inversely with rateable value per head. However, there is another suggestion to be made. The amount of relief accorded is difficult to calculate, as the proportion between indoor and outdoor relief will show. The table below throws some light on the question.

NUMBER OF PAUPERS IN ENGLAND AND WALES, 1895.

Divisions.	Indoor.		Outdoor.		Total.
	Number.	Number per 1000.	Number.	Number per 1000.	
South West.......	9,640	5·0	65,109	33·8	74,749
East	9,308	5·5	49,422	29·2	58,730
Welsh...........	6,763	3·6	54,087	29·0	60,850
West Midland....	20,342	6·1	72,551	21·7	92,893
North Midland....	7,749	4·1	43,683	23·2	51,432
South Midland....	9,610	4·8	44,538	22·2	54,148
Metropolis.......	62,554	14·3	51,481	11·7	114,035
South East.......	20,134	6·6	58,842	19·4	78,976
North	8,396	4·3	34,212	17·3	42,608
York	13,319	4·0	57,794	17·2	71,113
North West.......	30,017	6·1	62,032	12·6	92,049

The cost of indoor relief is as a rule much greater

than that of outdoor, yet we see that the Metropolis has
14'3 per 1,000 indoor paupers to 4'0 per 1,000 of York,
and 11'7 per 1,000 outdoor paupers to 17'2 of York,
that is, a total of 26 per 1,000 to a total of 21'2 per
1,000, and at the same time more than three times as
many indoor paupers per 1,000. The results of separate
unions and parishes would expose still greater contrasts.

Ignoring for the moment the principle of economy,
assuming in a word that administrations are equally
wise and economical, and that they will remain so
whatever financial assistance they receive, it is
immediately apparent that it is but common justice
that the poor law centre should be relieved of its
burden in proportion to the number of each kind of
paupers with which it deals per day. Pauperism is
much greater in some districts than in others. What
the present system comes to is that the poor alone
relieve the poor in many places. When the above
results are combined with those adopted with regard
to rateable value, it seems that outside contributions
for the relief of distress should, theoretically, vary
inversely as rateable value per head of the locality,
and directly as the quantity of indoor and outdoor
relief. The objection is the zealous supervision which
would be required to prevent wholesale waste, and an
alarming increase of pauperism. I am not so sure
that the magnitude of this danger is not largely
fictitious to-day; but in avoiding all appearance of
foolhardiness, and yet obtaining almost the like

effects, the system of paying constant costs which vary little with the quantity of pauperism out of funds obtained from large districts on the basis of rateable value is preferable. The Metropolitan Common Poor Fund exemplifies this system. This fund and the equalisation of rates fund constitute an exception to the allegation made at the beginning of this chapter that politicians have rather failed to recognise the diminution of responsibility with distance as regards the operations of local bodies. We have in the principles upon which these two funds are founded an instrument which will eject a good half of those puzzling inequities which trouble many a practical man and drive him to attach himself to the vague agitation for some reform of some character in local finances. Both these funds represent organised subventions, *which are not imperial but local*. In a word they are the systematisation of neighbourly, or provincial, assistance grounded on the admission of a large common responsibility. They mean a first step from the conception of society as made up of rigid, mutually exclusive, local units to that of an organic nation of organisms, whose size and strength and nature vary with function, and which come and go, expand and contract, with differences in the work set before them.

The Metropolitan Common Poor Fund, which was created in 1867, is administered by the Local Government Board. It is raised by a rate over the whole

Metropolitan district, excluding Penge, to meet certain costs incurred under the Poor Law, which are supposed not to vary at all considerably with efficiency of administration.[1]

The effect is, that the wealthier districts assist the

[1] Expenses to be paid out of Common Poor Fund by the Act of 1867.

1. Pauper lunatics.

2. Fever or smallpox patients in asylums.

3. Medicine, and medical- and surgical appliances supplied to those in receipt of relief.

4. All salaries and cost of rations of officers, managers of institutions and dispensers, provided the appointment of the officers is sanctioned by the Poor Law Board.

5. Compensation of medical officers of workhouses on the determination of their contract by the Poor Law Board, and of any officer who may be deprived of his office through this Act.

6. Fees for registration of births and deaths.

7. Fees and other expenses of vaccination.

8. Maintenance of pauper children in district, separate, certificated, and licensed schools.

9. For relief of destitute persons certified by the auditor, and for provision of temporary wards or other places of reception approved by the Poor Law Board, under the Metropolitan Houseless Poor Acts of 1864 and 1865.

"Additional items of expenditure have from time to time been cast upon the Fund. Thus, by the Metropolitan Poor Amendment Act, 1869, the cost of the maintenance of pauper boys on board training ships, and the cost of the maintenance and instruction of orphan and deserted children boarded out by the guardians, were made a charge upon the Fund. Under the Metropolitan Poor Amendment Act, 1870, the cost of the maintenance of adult paupers in workhouses and sick asylums to the extent of fivepence per head per day, and the cost of the rations of in-door officers according to a scale to be fixed by us became repayable out of the Fund. In 1873 the school fees paid by guardians for out-door pauper children were directed

poorer. In 1896 the net amount contributed was
£147,375, and the total expenditure charged to the
fund was £631,723 : 19 of the 31 districts received
in excess of their contributions, one district, St.
Saviour's, as much as £17,435. A wider application
has been given to the principle of the Metropolitan
Common Poor Fund by the passing of the London
(Equalisation of Rates) Act, 1894, by which each
parish contributes a rate of 6d. in the £ to a common
fund, which is expended in grants to sanitary
authorities on the basis of population.[1]

by the Elementary Education Act, 1873, to be paid out of the
Fund. In 1879 the expenses incurred by the managers of the
Metropolitan Asylum District in providing ambulances, ambul-
ance stations, and horses, and in respect of the persons
employed by them in the conveyance of persons suffering from
any dangerous infectious disease, were also charged upon the
Fund, and in 1889 the expenses incurred by the managers for
the maintenance of non-pauper patients suffering from fever or
small-pox or diphtheria, as well as pauper patients, were made
a charge upon the Fund. Payments are also made out of the
Fund in respect of the expenses of the Quarter Sessions for the
County of London under the Valuation (Metropolis) Act, 1869,
and the remuneration and expenses of the clerk and other
officers appointed to assist the Quarter Sessions; the fees
received by the Quarter Sessions under that Act being paid into
the Fund. The expenses of the Clerk to the London County
Council under the same Act are also payable out of the Fund."
(Report of Local Government Board for 1897-8.)

[1] The grants have to be spent as follows :
1. In works under the Public Health (London) Act, 1891.
2. The residue, if any, in respect of lighting.
3. The residue, if any, in respect of streets.
The population of the districts has to be estimated each year
from the number of houses.

The merit of these two funds is that the financial advantages of big districts are secured with the administrative advantages of small ones. The distribution of the funds, however, in both cases is not above criticism.

In the case of the Equalisation of Rates Fund, for instance, it is bad that population should determine the grants, for there is no guarantee that need is proportional to population, and not rateable value per head. Mr. Gomme has said, we may add, in his evidence to the present commission, that the population basis is not final; that it was taken as a first experiment to see how it would work out. Since, in these funds, we have in effect subventions between local bodies, we must beware of the dangers incidental to subventions, though, indeed, in these cases they are less, as the whole of the funds are raised in the locality.

CHAPTER VII

SUBVENTIONS IN ENGLAND PRIOR TO 1888

IMPERIAL subventions to local authorities are not peculiar to the British Isles ; they have appeared in some form in most modern civilised states.

In England the first of these grants was made in 1831, others followed in 1833 and 1835. Little was spent, however, until the time of the famous administration, whose claim to glory is the repeal of the Corn Laws. How far the repeal and subventions were connected in the mind of Sir Robert Peel is a matter of debate. It seems natural to suppose that the grants which came in 1846 were proposed to reconcile the landed interest to a measure which appeared to be striking heavily at it. Certainly, a few days after Sir Robert Peel had announced his conversion to Cobdenism, Lord Beaumont proposed a commission on the burdens of land on the ground that " protection " and " burdens " must live and die together ; but Mr. Gladstone assures us that he then voted for the commission and against Sir Robert Peel. But beyond a doubt the Free Trade Act of 1846 and subventions were associated by the landlords, and we know that the Anti-Corn-Law League was on the alert to check any attempt to re-adjust local taxation in the rural districts. In consequence, the Chancellor of the Exchequer, in the new government of 1851, announced that he was not going to recommend any change whatever in the system of raising the local taxes, and Cobden thereupon wrote to the chairman of the League : " The *Budget* has finally closed the controversy with Protection. Dizzy has in the most impudent way thrown over the ' local burdens,' as he did before a fixed duty. The League may be dissolved when you like."[1] In 1869 the Local Taxation Committee was formed out of the Central Chamber of Agriculture with the direct object of organising a crusade on the consolidated fund. The crusade was vigorously pursued and with marked success. In 1872 a motion for relief of the rates was carried in the House of Commons, and, although a motion practically identical was lost in 1884, it was carried again in 1886. Subventions rose from £1,420,183 in 1868 to £6,870,206 in 1888. The first amount, if spread evenly over the poor rate valuation of England and Wales, is equivalent to a rate of 3½d. in the £, the second to one of 11d. in the £.

All these subventions, with but few exceptions, were payments for work done, and were dependent on efficiency. And there is another point to be

[1] Morley's " Life of Cobden."

noticed besides the fact of the control of the central government, namely, that all these grants were made for the performance of local duties which were admittedly a part of the business of the Imperial Government. To such kinds of subsidy in general few objections can be made. Mr. G. H. Blunden says of them : " By coupling the grants [for police with the attainment of a fair standard of efficiency, much has been done in the past to increase the effectiveness and raise the character of the local forces. The grants for vaccination and registration have in like manner secured the performance of certain functions which would otherwise have been wholly neglected, or very imperfectly effected in a very large number of localities. The grant for main roads is fairly justified by the results secured, but the cost is heavy. The expenditure on sanitary officers is at present largely without result in many places, owing to the lax administration of the sanitary laws by the local governing bodies."[1] The local executive performs partially imperial duties, and it is paid for its work, not always the whole cost, but frequently only a definite proportion or a definite amount. For instance, only half the cost of the police was met from imperial funds, and even the half was dependent on satisfactory work ; and, again, in the case of disturnpiked and main roads, the proportion of the expense borne by the Exchequer was usually one

[1] " Local Taxation and Finance," p. 36.

quarter. In the case of the Dublin Police, however, the reverse system is in operation. The Imperial Government directly manages the corps, and receives from the Dublin Corporation the proceeds of a rate of 8d. in the £. But here we have an exceptional case.

The payment of a portion of the cost by the body undertaking any operation obviously stimulates economy, if the portion varies directly as the total cost. The system of part payment alone, however, would be insufficient to produce the most economical results, since the operations to which this system applied would tend to be carried beyond the point of maximum satisfaction, that is, the point at which marginal utility equalled marginal cost. This would result, because the cost to the locality which directly controlled the operations would be part only of the actual cost.

Suppose, for instance, that the marginal utility of 100 police in a locality is represented by £2 per man, and that the marginal utility of 120 police is represented by £1 per man, and suppose that in both cases the marginal supply price is £2 ; then if the locality paid the entire cost, 100 police would be employed ; but if the central government contributed half, 120 men would be employed. The engagement of the larger number may be prevented by imperial control other than financial ; and the difficulty was more of theoretical than of practical importance.

Another method of dividing cost is for the central government to pay, not a part of the total expenses, but the expenses of a part of the operations. The objection is that the expenses of this part will grow unchecked, and that other parts of the work will tend to become merged with the imperially paid portion, which will therefore become larger and more expensive than it was before. These tendencies require no proof. People both individually and in co-operation are notoriously careless as to expenses which they have not to meet. The Imperial Government adopted this method in dealing with the cost of poor relief, but the grants it made were practically unobjectionable, because only those costs were taken over, which are not to any appreciable extent dependent on efficiency. In the case of education, the central government pays a fixed amount per scholar and meets certain other expenses which need not be detailed here. It also makes additional payments to poor districts. All the education grants are accompanied by keen scrutiny, and the government keeps a tight hand on the reins of management.

Few blots on the system are to be detected. Education admittedly concerns more than the locality, and so a portion of the cost may not unreasonably be met from the Imperial Treasury. The advantages in the payment of a fixed sum is that efforts will be made by the school board, under pressure from the constituency, to reduce the balance, so far as reduction is consistent with efficiency, and perhaps a little further. The system of payment by results, exemplified by the South Kensington grants, has grave drawbacks in encouraging forcing, in overlooking the more subtle qualities in teaching, and in inducing excessively rigid systematization.

So far as the early subsidies [1] were made payable to rural districts, they had the undesirable effect of transferring a part of "the hereditary burden" on real property to the Exchequer. Further criticisms, which are common to these and to the later subventions, must be left to the close of the next chapter.

[1] A full detailed description of these subventions will be found in Appendix B to Mr. Fowler's " Report on Local Taxation."

CHAPTER VIII

THE SUBVENTION IN ENGLAND OF 1888 AND 1890

IN 1888, and again in 1890, came great changes. A new colour was given to subventions by grants being made the amount of which was not determined by the cost of specific work done, or by needs, but by the accidents governing the proceeds of given taxes. Mr. Fowler says: "The financial arrangements of the Local Government Act (1888) constituted a new departure from the principles on which Treasury subventions had previously been sanctioned by Parliament. On all previous occasions, except in the case of payments made by the Treasury in lieu of rates in respect of Government properties, the subventions annually voted had been allocated to specific purposes, to which it was considered that contributions might properly be made by the Exchequer; and their distribution had been regulated either by the expenditure in aid of which they are paid, or by the efficiency of work done by the local authorities or their officers. These principles were recognised by the Local Government Act, so far as the payments required to be made by the County and Borough Councils in substitution for the discontinued grants, were concerned; but they were disregarded as regards the application of the surplus remaining after the payments of these grants and the Union Officers Grant."[1]

The Local Government Act of 1888 transferred to the Councils of Counties and County Boroughs of England and Wales certain licenses, referred to in the Act as Local Taxation licenses, and a share of the Probate Duty. Certain of the old grants were charged on the new funds when the Act came into force. They were those in respect of Teachers in Poor Law Schools, Poor Law Medical Officers, the County, Borough, and Metropolitan Police, Public Vaccinators, Medical Officers of Health and Inspectors of Nuisances, Criminal Prosecutions, Pauper Lunatics, Registrars of Births and Deaths, Disturnpike and Main Roads, and Compensation to Clerks of the Peace. These grants were certified by the Local Government Board to have amounted for the year ending 31st of March, 1888, to £2,860,384.

The share of the Death Duties allocated to local authorities has varied from time to time. In 1888-9 one third of the Probate Duty was paid, in the years 1889-90 to 1893-94 one half of the Probate Duty, and in 1894-5 one half of the Probate Duty paid on the

[1] Report on Local Taxation, p. xlvii.

property of persons dying before the 2nd of August 1894, and also a share of the Estate Duty (1894) paid on the personal property of persons dying after 1st August 1894, such share being equivalent to one and a half per cent. on the net value of the property on which the Duty was leviable. The Act substituting the New Estate Duty for the Probate account and Old Estate Duty came into force on 1st August 1894, and now only the share of the Estate Duty mentioned above is paid into the Local Taxation Accounts.

In 1890 followed the sequel to the great change of 1888 in the form of the Local Taxation (Customs and Excise) Act, and the Customs and Inland Revenue Act. The latter of these Acts "imposed additional duties on spirits, and provided that the proceeds of these additional duties and the portion of the duties of excise and of customs in respect of beer" (namely, so much as will arise from duties of 3d. per barrel on beer and 6d. per gallon on spirits) "should be apportioned between England, Scotland and Ireland, and that the English share should be paid into the Local Taxation Account and appropriated as Parliament might by any Act passed in the same session direct. The Local Taxation (Customs and Excise) Act, 1890, contained provisions for the application of these duties. That Act provided that out of the amount paid into the Local Taxation Account for England in respect of these duties the sum of £300,000 should be applied for purposes of Police Superannuation, namely, £150,000 in aid of the Superannuation fund for the Metropolitan Police force, and £150,000 in aid of the superannuation of the other police forces in England (except the police force of the city of London). The residue of the proceeds of the duties was to be distributed between the counties and county boroughs as if it were part of the English share of the local taxation probate duty under the Local Government Act. The County Councils were enabled by the Act to apply the sum received by them in respect of these duties to technical education within the meaning of the Technical Instruction Act 1889, and in the case of any County to which the Welsh Intermediate Education Act, 1889, applied, towards intermediate and technical education under that Act."[1]

By the legislation of 1888 and 1890 a surplus of more than £3,000,000, over and above the discontinued grants, was handed over to the English County Councils and County Boroughs. A new grant, however, to Boards of Guardians for Union Officers,[2]

[1] Mr. Fowler's "Report on Local Taxation."

[2] The Union Officers' Grant, amounting to about one million pounds, was given to a rate which was steadily falling, and which, moreover, had already been relieved by no less than four Treasury subventions, exclusive of the Grant for awards to public vaccinators, namely, the grants for (1) teachers in poor law schools, (2) poor law medical officers, (3) pauper lunatics, and (4) registrars of births and deaths.

amounting to £967,793 was charged upon this surplus. The distribution of the funds under the new Acts is wonderfully complicated.

The problem is divided into two stages; firstly division between the counties ;[1] and secondly, division in each County between its own Council and the County Borough Councils contained within its borders.

With respect to distribution between counties, in the first place the licenses are divided according to the amounts collected in each county. The rest of the grants are then added together, and from them are deducted the new allowances for police super-annuation.[2] The residue is then divided among the counties in proportion to the shares which the Local Government Board certified to have been received by each county[3] out of the discontinued grants during the year which ended on the 31st of March, 1888.

[1] The following are treated as separated counties under the Act : Ridings of Yorkshire ; Divisions of Lincolnshire ; East and West divisions of Sussex ; East and West divisions of Suffolk ; Isle of Ely ; Residue of Cambridge ; Soke of Peter-borough ; Residue of Northampton. The Metropolis also, which is further subject to special regulations.

[2] Another small sum may also be deducted, for, if in any financial year the money standing to the Cattle Pleuro-Pneumonia Account is insufficient to defray the costs of the execution of the Act of 1890 in Great Britain, the Local Government Board have to pay out of the Local Taxation Account such additional sums as the Board of Agriculture certify to be required.

[3] " In the case of the six counties of South Wales and the Isle

We have to consider next the distribution of the grants to each county between the County Council and the County Borough Councils. Commissioners were appointed to make equitable adjustments. It was said by Mr. Ritchie, when President of the Local Government Board, in reply to questions on the 3rd of July, 1888, that "the Government desired as far as possible that the boroughs should have the same control over their license duties as that which was given to the counties," and again that "the instruction to the commission was that regard should be had to the amount derived from license duties." The Act of 1888, however, in referring to the adjustments, has it, "that the county is not to be placed in any worse financial position by reason of the boroughs therein being constituted county boroughs, and that a county borough is not to be placed in any worse financial position than it would have been in if it had remained part of the county." The Commissioners found it impossible to discover any means of carrying out the intention of the latter clause, since all the surpluses (left after payment of the grants charged to the allocated taxes) would, had there been no county boroughs, have gone to swell the general purposes account of each county fund.

of Wight add also the amount which each of said counties and the Isle of Wight would have received if the roads maintained by the County Roads Boards or the Highway Commissioners had been main roads." (Act of 1888.)

It was a matter of doubt how far each borough would
have benefited from the expenditure of the surpluses,
especially as the whole cost of the maintenance of
main roads had to be defrayed by the County Council
as a general county purpose, and the Borough
Councils might have been able to obtain recogni-
tion of some roads within the borough as main
roads. The Commissioners state in their report that
they decided that an equitable adjustment would
be effected "by giving to such several authorities
in each year the annual amount received prior to
the passing of the Local Government Act out of
the grants discontinued after the passing of that
Act, together with the amount payable under . . .
section 26" (payments to guardians in respect of the
cost of Union Officers), "and dividing the remainder
in proportion to the rateable values of the county
and boroughs." But Mr. Wharton, a member of
the Commission, declares that "the Commissioners did not adopt the principle of rateable
value as their guide. They adopted the principle
of rateable value and population."[1] The award of
the Commissioners stands for five years. After that
period the whole question may be reopened by
appeal.

Both methods of division, that between the counties
and that between the county boroughs, are open to

[1] See question 10,273 before Commission on Local Taxation,
now sitting.

severe criticism. Take, firstly, division between the counties. In so far as it relates to the probate, estate, and beer and spirit duties, its basis is irrational. There is no reason why the Empire's contributions to the counties, to be largely spent on technical education in all probability, should vary, *inter alia*, with the numbers of people vaccinated and of inspectors of nuisances in the year 1887-8. There is no rational connection between a county's claim on the Imperial Exchequer in 1898 and its band of pauper lunatics in the year 1887-8. No thought was taken for different rates of growth in the counties in the future. As Mr. Hulton put it "when the Act was passed the distribution . . . might be right and proper, but after the lapse of nine years a distribution based on an accidental state of things in a previous year seems anomalous, and ought to be reconsidered."[1] Obviously, if the old grants for specific purposes had been continued, the counties which have grown in population would now be receiving larger proportions of the whole, so that if the basis were right in 1887-8 it must be wrong now, and it will every year become more and more wrong. The favoured counties are, of course, acquiring a vested interest in the ratio of 1887-8, and the more absurd it becomes the more difficult it will be to overthrow it."[2]

[1] Memorandum handed into present Commission, c. 8765, page 114.

[2] Mr. Edwin Cannan in a letter to the *Manchester City News*, March 8th, 1899.

In Appendix VII. the amounts of the discontinued grants, the shares received, and rateable values for the counties of England and Wales, are given. In the last two columns the enormous difference between the existing distribution and one based on rateable value is shewn. Side by side with this Appendix VI. should be studied. It shows that a distribution on the basis of population would also give results widely different to those brought about by existing arrangements.

We may now pass on to a consideration of the principle by which the division of the residue of the grants between the county borough councils and the county councils was regulated. If in division of the proceeds of the licences between counties the simple and obvious principle of giving to each its own was satisfactory, it is difficult to understand why it was not sufficiently satisfactory for a final subdivision. As it is, the basis adopted, whatever it was, has compelled almsgiving, in many cases by the poorest to the wealthiest. Appendix V. shows that the excess of receipts over contributions has amounted to as much as £23,058 5s. od. (in Manchester) and deficiencies to £13,601 17s. 1od. (in the County of Lancaster). Excesses and deficits amounted together to £184,211 12s. 2d. in 1896. Division, there is little doubt, was largely made on the basis of rateable value. Therefore, if there are two boroughs with equal populations, and alike in all respects, except that the one is rich and the other poor, the richer receives the greater amount.

An instructive commentary on existing distribution, both between counties and afterwards between counties and county boroughs, will be found in Appendix VI. We find there that the shares of the doles of 1890 amounted in 1896 to 10·1d. per head in London, 10·3d. in Bootle, 3·1d. in Walsall, and 4·5d. in Durham, to take a few examples.

Distribution of the residues is made on the basis of poor rate assessment, in so far as rateable value is taken into account. Now the poor rate assessments are made in one county by many different bodies with different ideas. Moreover, different rates of reduction are used in obtaining rateable value from gross estimated rental. Sheffield, for instance, allows 20 to 25 per cent on houses and shops, while Bradford allows only 15 per cent. On stone quarries Burnley deducts 15 per cent., and Prescot makes no deduction at all.

The county rate valuation is made by one body, and the system upon which it is based is therefore uniform throughout the county. When we compare it with the valuations of the assessment committees of the Unions the differences are seen to vary considerably, as we should naturally expect from the foregoing facts. Here they are for a few picked parishes in East Sussex in 1895.

Poor Rate Assessment.	County Rate Basis.	Percentage below County Rate Basis.
£359,149	£368,202	2·458
111,006	115,234	3·669
100,288	108,980	7·975
312,614	363,351	13·963
63,230	76,957	17·837
58,363	73,721	20·832

(From Vol. I., part ii., page 116, of the Minutes of Evidence of the present Commission.)

Moreover, it is not the easiest matter in the world to get the poor rate valuation revised. It cost Walsall seven years of agitation.

It follows directly, of course, that the distribution of the residue of grants on the basis of poor rate valuation must be in cases extremely inequitable, even supposing that true rateable value would be an equitable basis.

The method of distributing the present subventions is indeed hopelessly casual. Mr. Cannan's "the thimble-rig of exchequer contributions"[1] exactly describes it.

Quite apart from their foolish distribution the grants of 1888 and 1890 are objectionable for many other reasons. Take the licenses for instance. They are raised in the counties; the central government imposes and collects them ; the counties receive them. It would be preferable if the clause in the Act which provides for their collection by the recipients, when

[1] *Economic Journal*, Vol. IV., p. 26.

decreed by order in Council, had been carried out, as the fatal stamp of "dole" would then have been removed. The allocation of certain taxation bases, in their entirety, to the complete control of the local bodies, if some assistance really was needful, would have been even more preferable. Nevertheless, of the imperial contributions in and after 1888 the duties on licenses are the least objectionable as they are collected from the beneficiaries. They simply mean borrowing half-a-crown from a friend for the purpose of making him a present of it. Some may object to them because they do not vary with expenditure. If they were still destined for the Imperial Exchequer, it may be argued, they would tend to vary in rate with the Exchequer's wants. But this point is not of much importance since a barometer of expenditure is as a rule sufficient, and local rates provide it.

Passing from the licenses to the other grants in the later period we find cause for disapprobation in the fact that the areas of collection and distribution are not coterminous. For the moment there seems to be nothing portentous in the fact, but it soon becomes apparent that it means no guarantee that the proceeds of the allocated taxes will tend to vary as the needs of the recipients, when growth alone is taken into consideration. Very much in the rough, we may put the situation thus. When a tax is imposed by a governing body on its own constituents, then doubling the constituents doubles the financial needs of the

Government, but it doubles also the receipts. But collect a tax from the nation at large and pay the results to a locality; then, although the constituents of the locality may increase in numbers, and its needs may therefore increase, the proceeds of the tax need not increase, since the nation as a whole may have diminished.

For example, Manchester's needs vary as its population, but its allocated taxes, excepting only duties on licenses, do not vary with its population. The natural and rational thing is for mere movements in population not to affect taxation burdens. But they do, as regards local imposts, now that the reforms of 1888 and 1890 are in force. Another very insidious element of chance has been screwed into local finances, and improvidence must therefore be cheerfully awaited. An element of chance accompanied the earlier subventions. Their most harmful effects followed rather from the manner in which they were accorded than directly from them. Harried governments took to casting sops in the shape of subventions. The outcome was inevitable. The assumption of certain charges was innocent enough, comparatively speaking, but the hap-hazard manner of the assumptions, and their seemingly time-serving character, gave rise to a sanguine uncertainty. It was the unexpectedness of the doles which created the great expectations whose outcome was waste: it is so much easier to agitate for help than to manage not

to need it. The allocated millions of 1890 were
simply windfalls, nothing more nor less, with the dust
and ashes within almost concealed. The money was
collected for the payment of compensation for sup-
pressed liquor licenses, of which the House of
Commons stubbornly refused to approve, and when
that object was dropt the money had to be expended
in some other way. It was proposed by the Government to leave it ear-marked in the Treasury for a
time, but the Speaker held that, in view of the budget,
it would be illegal not to spend it in the same year.
Hence the compulsory decision to throw it after the
grants of 1888. There was no conviction of need
and no prior design. Special circumstances are
claimed in justification of the grants of 1888. In
that year new bodies with large powers were called
into being; or, more correctly, some ancient institutions were revived and given a modern dress.[1] Their
fate hung in the balance. They might become mere
excrescences, lifeless aggregations of inefficiency.
Granting their enthusiasm, their aspirations might
easily be checked on the financial side by the murmurs
of an already overburdened constituency. The new
bodies must be sent forth with the strength of an
assured revenue. If income frequently tends to considerably exceed expenditure a governmental body
may find itself branching out in new directions,

[1] A few years later came the Parish Councils Bill with promise
of further financial pressure.

assuming new functions, and hurrying along new paths, as the most progressive of progressivists. " New occasions teach new duties." Ways must be found to spend the balances. True, American expenditure of surplus revenues seems to have been unfortunate, but this was perhaps due to the adoption of the costly and scandalous pension system, which, like the young cuckoo, soon ousted all competitors. Certainly adverse balances are a check on hasty decisions ; yet it is possible for a public body to hurry too little, and it may be wise on occasion to stimulate it at the temporary sacrifice of economy. It is alleged that subventions, especially the allocated taxes, have applied a much-needed stimulus ; that the burden of rates was checking the development of local government, and that the new funds removed this check.

We have been told that there is a very practical example of the value of largess in the effect of the surpluses ear-marked for technical instruction. Mr. G. H. Blunden says :—" The grants for technical instruction and intermediate education have only existed since 1890, but they are rapidly building up a great and excellent work, which, although much needed, was likely to have remained undone without the stimulus and aid thus afforded. In both directions a vast amount of voluntary effort and public spirit has been evoked, which only needs wise direction to ensure excellent results before long."[1] But educational specialists present to us the reverse of the view offered by Mr. Blunden. They point out that there is a mist enveloping technical education which prevents a clear presentation of its nature to the untrained intellect, and that on this account alone much money has been foolishly disbursed. Too large a proportion of the funds has flowed into already swollen channels, and many streams of equal importance, and whose need is greater, have been left to dry up. Hence the proposed Bill drawn up by the Head Masters' Association, and founded on the conviction that the existing elective bodies are incapable of judiciously disposing of these funds without assistance from educational specialists. Perhaps the educational question is a peculiar one. But, however that may be, we have here the advantages and disadvantages contrasted: on the one side "a great and excellent work," on the other, waste and the misdirection of much expenditure.[2]

How shall the two sides be balanced? This is a hard question, but one conclusion at least is certain, namely, that if any unconditioned grant is made it must be only temporary. We are then face to face with the difficult problem as to when a temporary

[1] "Local Taxation and Finance," p. 36.
[2] The objection above noted applies only in the present. Educational wisdom is finding its way to the boards of local governments.

support is to be removed. If history affords any guidance, a temporary support tends to become a permanency; partly because of opposition from the vested interest created by the support. The policy of protecting infant industries has split upon this rock, and there is no reason to suppose that a policy of temporary subsidies will be more fortunate. The two sides, however, need not be balanced. The present murmurings about the burden of the rates are directed entirely to defects in the existing system which are removable.

It has been seriously questioned whether sub-ventions have relieved rates at all. It is urged that they cannot, as rates have not fallen. In proof an appeal is made to statistics. It is pointed out that in England and Wales subventions amounted to 3½d. in the pound in 1868, 11d. in 1888, and 1s. 6¼d. in 1892; and that rates in the pound were, in 1868, 3s. 4d., in 1880, 3s. 3⅛d., in 1888, 3s. 7⅓d., in 1891, 3s. 7⅓d., and in 1893, 3s. 9⅓d. The only fall was between 1868 and 1880, and then it only amounted to one-fifth of a penny. The inference we are in-tended to draw, apparently, is that the subventions have been wasted. Now the figures will not support this conclusion. Firstly, there is no proof that rates would not have increased more if there had been no subventions. We cannot even fall back for proof on an average increase in rates, as many changes have been introduced into local government which affect rates. The enormous change of 1888, for instance, cuts off the years succeeding from those preceding that time. There is another alternative to the conclusion above, which is that the new funds have been swallowed up in new functions, or in old functions more efficiently performed. Besides, the facts are really not quite as they are represented in the above argument. If allowance were made for variations in the purchasing power of money, a fall, both in total rates and in rates per head, in 1888 would probably appear. The use of Sauerbeck's index numbers at any rate shows it. Rates, in fact, did not resume their natural rate of growth again till 1892.

CHAPTER IX

THE AGRICULTURAL RATINGS BILL

THE Agricultural Ratings Bill raises two distinct questions. The one, Is farming as a business over-taxed for local purposes? The other, Have the hereditary burdens on the land increased, and if so ought the landlords to be compensated? By the hereditary burdens is meant those which are fixed to the land by the diminution which they cause in its value through amortisation, that is, those which fall ultimately on the landlord in possession at the time of their imposition.

With regard to the first question, it has already been said that an investigation into the quantity of productive work (including transport) performed by local bodies in the performance of local operations, with reference to different businesses (including agriculture), and a careful estimation of the costs of those services regarded as productive, is a pressing need, and, moreover, an essential step preliminary to reform in local taxation. It is a labour requiring the co-operation of experts thoroughly representative of the multitudinous business concerns of this country.

It is not denied here, though it certainly is not taken as established, that the business of agriculture suffers especial hardship. What is denied is that the inquisition of commissions has been such as to provide the evidence to justify a categorical statement upon the matter. Moreover, we must remember that concessions have been already made to the farming interest by the Lighting and Watching Act of 1833, and by the series of sanitary and improvement Acts which commenced in 1848. "Watching and lighting rates under the first mentioned Act are chargeable only on one-third of the full rate in the pound, when levied in respect of land and tithes; lines of railway and canals being comprehended under the term 'lands.' Sanitary rates in urban districts, and those for special sanitary purposes in rural districts, are chargeable in respect of agricultural land, tithes, railways,[1] docks, and canals, on one quarter only of the rateable value."[2] No such concession is made as regards borough rates, although much of the expenditure to which the proceeds are applied is of a similar character.

Turning from the business aspect to that of the burdens on land, we find ourselves in a far less helpless position. That portion of the average rates of the last fifty years or so which fall on the landlord

[1] In urban districts in which the repair of highways has been taken over by the counties, the expenditure is now charged on land and railways in full, instead of at one-fourth as heretofore.

[2] Blunden, Op. cit., p. 25.

H

have, by amortisation, become a fixed charge in the land—"an hereditary burden," as Mr. Fowler expresses it. Lands have been bought and sold subject to this charge : the tax was paid for all time by the owner when the rates were imposed. A remission now would therefore be in very many cases a free gift to those who have contributed nothing. But it is urged that rents are falling—this is the popular form that the argument takes, and it was the form current at the time of the great increase in subventions, after the repeal of the Corn Laws. But the Government is not responsible for the rise or fall in rents, and the landlord has (or should have) taken into consideration average and foreseen rates in his purchase. No Government would hearken unto a speculator for the rise who claimed assistance because of the fall in the stock in which he operated ; and what if the stock be land !

But a claim has been entered for relief with re-ference only to the increase of rates. Now, if there were an increase, it would be incumbent upon us to investigate with a view to discovering whether as much value had been given to the land by the services of local bodies as was taken away in the form of rates. But a wide review reveals no appreci-able increase, if increase at all. It will be seen from the following figures that the actual charges on land, and the charges per pound, have decreased since 1868, and very greatly since the beginning of the century.

(Compiled from figures given in Fowler's Report on Local Taxation.)

Local Rates Borne by Lands (including Gardens, etc., exceeding one acre).	Value of Land (from Income Tax Valuations).	Rate per £ on Lands.
		Shillings.
1817 . . . . £6,730,000	(1814) £37,063,000	3·63
1868 5,500,000	— 47,767,000	2·3
1891 4,260,000	— 42,234,872	2·02

On pages 116 and 117 tables are given showing that although the amount of the urban and rural rates has augmented since 1868 by about one quarter, and that of the rural rates by a little more in the same period, yet the rate in the pound of these rates has fallen. There is an advance in the rate for the rural sanitary authorities, but this is offset by a considerable fall in the poor rate.

Now all that is contended is that the evidence of loss is not sufficiently convincing to justify a national gift to the landlords. In support of the contention, here are two quotations from Mr. Fowler's Report :—

" The burdens of Local Taxation on lands were found in 1868 to be not heavier than they had been at various periods of the century, nor so heavy as in most foreign countries."[1] Again : " If in the distribution of Treasury subventions an undue share of any grants was awarded to the rural districts, the result would be that the owners of agricultural lands

[1] Report, p. 51.

AMOUNTS RECEIVED FROM RATES BY THE VARIOUS LOCAL AUTHORITIES

(Compiled from Fowler's Report, pp. 6 and 7, Appendix A, and from Report of Local Government Board).

	1868.	1873-4.	1879-80.	1887-8.	1890-1.	1893-4.
Urban Metropolitan	3,702,833	4,024,757	5,339,774	6,983,757	7,929,946	8,999,465
Extra ,, ...	3,027,154	4,744,452	6,193,308	8,855,220	9,583,684	10,424,821
Total............	6,729,987	8,769,209	11,523,082	15,838,977	17,513,630	19,424,286
Urban and Rural	8,357,765	8,420,077	8,579,347	9,476,990	8,546,991	10,724,224 [1]
Rural............	1,415,685	1,716,851	2,057,170	1,878,869	1,758,021	2,075,462
Total of Urban and Rural, and Rural....	9,773,450	10,136,938	10,637,017	11,355,859	10,305,012	12,799,686
Total of all rates............	16,503,437	18,906,137	22,160,099	27,194,836	27,818,642	32,223,972

[1] These figures include the School Board rate of rural districts, as the reports of the Committee of Council on Education do not distinguish the amounts received in rural from those received in extra-Metropolitan urban districts other than boroughs. It has been ascertained, however, that for 1890-1 £350,652 belongs to the rural rates. This amount is just less than half the sum for the two districts together, viz., £772,013.

RATES IN THE POUND FOR VARIOUS LOCAL AUTHORITIES
(Compiled from Fowler's Report, Appendix A, and from Report of Local Government Board).

	1873-4.	1879-80.	1887-8.	1890-1.	1893-4.
Urban Metropolitan— Rate in £ of Rates raised by all Local Authorities, calculated on Poor Rate Valuation	3. 11'3	4. 4'3	4. 6'6	5. 0'2	5. 4'0
Extra Metropolitan— Rate in £ of Rates raised by purely Urban Extra Metropolitan Authorities	2. 4'8	2. 4'1	2. 8'6	2. 10'2	
Urban and Rural Poor Law Authorities— (Extra Metropolitan)	1. 4'4	1. 1'4	1. 1'0	10'9	10'8
County Authorities— County Rate	2'7	2'3	2'5	2'3	
Police Rate	2'4 .	1'8	1'9	2'0	
Other Rates			0'5		
Rural— Sanitary Authorities			1'5	1'9	2'4
Highway ,,	6'9	7'7	6'9	6'0	6'9

would derive a greater advantage than the occupiers of houses in urban districts."[1]

In 1896 the Agricultural Land Ratings Bill was forced on a protesting House. It dealt with certain rates on agricultural land ; and it was based upon an interim report of the Royal Commission on Agricultural Depression. The Bill declared that the rates to which it applied should only be half as much on agricultural land as on houses.[2] The Commission

[1] Ibid., p. 41.
[2] This involved the valuation of the land apart from the farmhouse.

had suggested that lands should be charged on only a quarter of their rateable value ; but the exigencies of the Government forced it to adopt the proportion of one-half. The deficit in local revenues was to be made good out of the Imperial Exchequer. It was estimated at £970,000 for 1896, and £1,950,000 for succeeding years. The amount was to be divided between England, Scotland, and Ireland in the proportions of 80 per cent., 11 per cent., and 9 per cent. The Bill met with the most violent and sustained opposition, and the closure had to be persistently applied to get it through.

It was denied that the money would go into the pockets of the landlords. Against this view we may instance evidence,[1] brought forward in the course of debate, which showed that landlords were even then taking the relief into account in estimating reductions in rents. The discussion in Chapter V. of this essay makes it evident that the relief accorded at the margin will ultimately benefit the consumers, but that the difference between this and the amounts remitted will ultimately go (in great part) to the landlords. In the meanwhile, however, farmers will receive benefits, but in different degrees, as the Earl of Rosebery was careful to point out during the debate in the House of Lords. Those farming the more expensive lands will receive the biggest doles. That this should be so is not only unfair, but it

[1] See Hansard, also Annual Register.

means also that the very object of the Bill is defeated, for the cloud of depression hangs more heavily over the low rent lands—for instance, over Essex.

We may put the several objections to this piece of legislation as follows :—Little relief was given where the Commission showed it was needed most, and much was given where it was not needed. The amount of the doles was determined by imperial surpluses and not by needs. The division of spoils between the heads of the Empire was practically arbitrary. A free gift was made incidentally to some landlords.

The Bill is to continue in operation for five years. An attempt to cut down the period to three years proved unsuccessful. It has been welcomed in certain quarters, but the welcome is almost drowned in a clamour for more : for example, the following is part of a resolution passed unanimously by the Central and Associated Chambers of Agriculture on May the 5th, 1896 :—

" That this Council welcomes and approves the Agricultural Land Ratings Bill as a *partial* measure of relief, but *regrets* that it does not reduce the assessment of agricultural land to one-fourth, as suggested by this Council." (The italics are mine.)

CHAPTER X

SUMMARY AND CONCLUSION

THE practical conclusions arrived at in this essay
may be expressed in the three following proposi-
tions.

I. The subventions to which the local governments
in this country have been subjected were not all
equally objectionable. Some were less desirable than
others. Some offended against many financial and
political principles, and some against only a few.
The subsidies accorded prior to 1888 assumed on the
whole the least objectionable shape possible, but
among them also there were degrees of defects. The
subventions of 1888 and 1890 ran counter to most
principles which the statesman should hold in mind
in directing legislation of this kind, and their division
between counties, and between counties and county
boroughs, was even more unreasonable.

II. Even if the burden of the rates, and the
injustices committed in their imposition, be admitted,
and also the lethargy of local bodies, both the old

and the newborn, in consequence of difficulties in raising funds, and even if it be assumed that the fundamental evils (*i.e.*, the burden and inequity of the rates) are irremovable, yet the policy of subventions is a very doubtful policy. Those who argue that subsidies bring more troubles than they remove have a strong case. Nevertheless, it must be granted that the balancing of advantages and disadvantages under these assumptions is a matter of the greatest difficulty.

III. But the arguments in Chapters IV., V., and VI. clearly show that no such balancing of utilities and drawbacks is needful, because the fundamental evils in the existing system of raising local finances are not essential but chiefly accidental and removable. The opinion was expressed that a system of local taxation, as nearly perfect as any system can be, might be constructed. In the light of this belief most subsidies stand absolutely condemned, as panaceas with some disagreeable accompaniments for troubles which might be directly removed. But some subsidies escape this condemnation, those, namely, which follow upon the division of governmental labour between the various governments in the nation, (Chapter II.). The rules by which such subsidies should be governed are outlined in Chapter III. It must be carefully borne in mind that in practically all these cases the obligation to contribute to the cost of local services

diminishes with distance from the locality. In a
word, it must not be forgotten that a nation is a
hierarchy of social organisms constituted by civic
feeling.

APPENDIX A

THE EFFECT OF SUBVENTIONS ON THE QUANTITY [1] AND INCIDENCE OF TAXATION

THE sole excuse for this Appendix is that the question with which it deals has been gravely discussed.

Let us clearly understand what it is we are attempting to estimate. The problem has been expressed as the effect of subventions on the quantity and incidence of taxation. Now it is at once apparent that such a problem is insoluble; for expressed otherwise it becomes, to find the differences in the quantity and incidence of taxation between present conditions, of which subventions are a part, and conditions which would have been had subventions not been given. When the question is thrown into this shape, we see at once that an answer is impossible, for we have no means of knowing what the conditions without subventions would have been.

[1] This is treated to some extent in Chapter VIII.

It is possible, indeed, to overcome the difficulty by making the violent assumptions that, had the sub-ventions not been introduced, the same funds would have been required by the local authorities as in the previous year, and that they would have been raised in the same manner, and that the amount of imperial funds raised would have been the same, less the sub-ventions, as in the year in question. But it would be folly to conduct an investigation vitiated by such wild·hypotheses.

Again, it is possible to overcome the difficulty by assuming that the total amount raised by local and imperial taxation would be the same under both con-ditions—therefore the first part of the question, as to "quantity," must be begged—and that the difference in incidence will be the difference between the incidence of the amount of the subventions, if raised on the basis of imperial taxes, and the incidence of this sum if raised by an increase in rates. But these hypotheses, big as they are, are not big enough. What is meant by the expression, "raised on the basis of imperial taxes"? It might mean perhaps— Mr. W. A. Hunter[1] gives it this meaning apparently —if raised in a manner least advantageous to the working-classes. Why not indeed, we may ask, in a manner most advantageous to the working-classes, or in any manner we choose to imagine? Mr. Hunter's hypothesis is truly "a very bold one" as

[1] *Contemporary Review*, Oct., 1893.

Mr. W. H. Smith[1] suggests. It may be urged that
the imperial system of taxation must be taken as a
whole, and that therefore "raised on the basis of
imperial taxes" must mean distributed over all
the taxes in proportion to their yield. If we
acted on this interpretation, then the effect of the
subventions on the incidence of taxation would be
the difference between the incidence of their amount,
if raised by rates, and the incidence of the imperial
taxes, divided by the amount of their yield, and
multiplied by the amount of the subventions. If we
worked this out we might find that subventions had
raised a burden from the classes which escape income
tax. But a detailed investigation would be wasted
labour as the suppositions worked up in the reason-
ing would render the results worthless.

But, to follow another line of thought under the
direction of the assumptions previously made, the
expression, "raised on the basis of imperial taxes,"
might mean "as the subventions actually are raised."
Here seems light at last. But it proves to be only a
Will o' the Wisp leading to the slough of fallacy.
Subventions may take the form of specific taxes ear-
marked for the local authorities, or they may not.
If they do not, then how are they actually raised ?
If they do, then they may be old taxes ; and if so,
the effect of the subventions is obviously not identical

[1] *Economic Journal*, Vol. V., p. 190.

with the effect of these old taxes, but with *the effect of the operations whereby, after payment of the subventions, imperial revenue and expenditure are again brought together.* Developing this idea, we might assume that the operations mentioned are increases in taxation, and that increases to the amount of the subventions would not have been imposed but for the introduction of the subventions. But we need not make this assumption. The operations whereby imperial expenditure and revenue are again brought together are not bound to be on the side of revenue at all; they might consist in reduced expenditure. And even if equilibrium were restored from the side of revenue, the cause need not be an increase of taxes. It might be a spontaneous increase in the proceeds of existing taxes. But assuming that expenditure and revenue again balance, and that taxes have been increased to bring about this result, yet the proceeds of the increases in taxation may be less or more than the amount of the subventions : if they are less, what can we say of the difference ? if they are more, which find their origin in the new expenditure on subventions, and which in decreased revenue, or increased expenditure, in other directions ? Again, if the operations, whereby balance is restored in the accounts, consist in a spontaneous increase in the proceeds of certain taxes, what is the effect of the subventions? We can only say that it is the difference between the effect of taxes as they are and the effect of taxes as they would have been, if subventions had not been. This only throws us back on a difficulty already treated : What would have been if the subventions had not been? If taxes would have been reduced, in which taxes would the reduction have taken place?

We are led to the conclusion before stated, that no solution is possible.

UNIVERSITY OF CALIFORNIA

STATISTICAL APPENDICES

TABLE I.

(Compiled from Mr. Fowler's Report on Local Taxation, 1893.)

A. PARLIAMENTARY GRANTS IN AID OF LOCAL RATES.

Grants in aid of	When first voted.	1867-68.	1877-88.	1891-92.
Teachers in Poor Law Schools ..	1846	£34,500	£36,825	..
Poor Law Medical Officers	1846	104,500	149,506	..
Police (Counties and Boroughs) ..	1856	225,300	861,083	..
Metropolitan Police	1833	164,848	575,141	£4,300
Criminal Prosecutions..	1835	150,000	133,732	..
County and Borough Prisons and Removal of Convicts..	1835 and 1846	109,000	..	..
Metropolitan Fire Brigade	1865-66	10,000	10,000	10,000
Berwick Bridge	1831	90	90	90
Industrial Schools (Local Authorities)	1876	3,574	32,212	38,800
Elementary Education (School Boards) Fee Grant	1891	..	..	329,285
Annual Grants for Day and Evening Scholars	1870	..	1,255,938	1,508,427
School Boards in Poor Districts ∴	1870	..	7,167	8,395
Medical Officers of Health and Inspectors of Nuisances	1873-74	..	73,910	..
Pauper Lunatics	1874	..	485,109	..
Registration of Births and Deaths ..	1875	..	9,500	..
Disturnpike and Main Roads ..	1882	..	498,797	..
Total (carried forward)		£301,512	£4,132,070	£1,899,297

TABLE I.—*Continued.*

B. LOCAL CHARGES TRANSFERRED TO, AND OTHER CHARGES OF A LOCAL
NATURE BORNE BY, ANNUAL VOTES OF PARLIAMENT.

Charges in respect of	When first voted.	1867-68.	1887-88.	1891-92.
District Auditors	1846	£17,900	£15,246	£14,069
Clerks of Assize	1852	18,500	19,602	17,975
Compensation to Clerks of Peace, etc.	1855	6,400	1,806	198
Central Criminal Court	1846	..	5,181	..
Middlesex Sessions	1859-60	..	819	1,454
Public Vaccinators	1867	6,000	16,468	..
Elementary Education (Voluntary Schools) Fee Grant	1891	..	..	493,155
Annual Grants for Day and Evening Scholars	1854	443,345	1,927,285	2,089,473
Reformatory Schools	1854-55	} 99,426	{ 66,920	62,365
Industrial Schools (other than those of Local Authorities)	1856-57		103,667	109,026
Rates on Government Property ..	1859	27,000	182,459	192,344
County and Burgh Prisons and Removal of Convicts	1879	..	398,683	398,047
Pleuro-Pneumonia	1890	..	..	140,000
Total		£618,571	£2,738,136	£3,518,106
Carried forward from previous page		£801,512	£4,132,070	£1,899,297
Total Parliamentary Subventions, excluding Allocated Taxes.. ..		£1,420,083	£6,870,206	£5,417,403

All the Education Grants are not included in the above tables, for instance, the
Science and Art (South Kensington) Grants are omitted. The total grants for education
(including everything) made to schools in England and Wales in 1897-8 amounted to
£4,501,895, and of this sum £3,597,496 went to Board Schools.

TABLE II.

(From Fowler's Report on Local Taxation.)

	Parliamentary Grants in aid of Local Rates.	Local Charges transferred to, and other charges of a Local Nature borne by, Annual Votes of Parliament.		Parliamentary Grants in aid of Local Rates.	Local Charges transferred to, and other Charges of a Local Nature borne by, Annual Votes of Parliament.
1868.	£801,512	£618,571	1881.	£2,733,993	£2,450,101
1869.	866,082	721,339	1882.	2,857,403	2,455,390
1870.	902,317	800,904	1883.	3,170,983	2,529,525
1871.	901,333	872,417	1884.	3,380,808	2,623,905
1872.	925,590	1,088,474	1885.	3,523,418	2,607,742
1873.	938,965	1,169,368	1886.	3,658,746	2,681,760
1874.	1,088,416	1,214,867	1887.	3,767,096	2,715,164
1875.	1,623,366	1,330,203	1888.	4,132,070	2,738,136
1876.	2,115,809	1,526,812	1889.	4,891,548	2,797,384
1877.	2,268,641	1,635,036	1890.	6,312,936	2,778,868
1878.	2,469,408	1,802,664	1891.	7,485,875	2,924,224
1879.	2,540,043	2,329,878	1892.	8,328,376	3,518,106
1880.	2,636,096	2,434,651			

TABLE III.

PAYMENTS TO LOCAL TAXATION ACCOUNTS.

Years ending 31st March.	PAYMENTS TO LOCAL TAXATION ACCOUNTS OUT OF:—				PAID TO LOCAL TAXATION ACCOUNTS.		
	Additional Beer and Spirit Duties.	Licenses.	Share of Probate Duty and of Estate Duty (1894).	Total.	England.	Scotland.	Ireland.
1889 ..	..	..	£1,400,000	£1,400,000	£1,120,000	£154,000	£126,000
1890 ..	..	£2,970,000	2,215,520	5,185,520	4,748,416	240,167	196,947
1891 ..	£1,235,592	3,334,419	2,404,401	6,974,412	5,947,613	700,988	325,881
1892 ..	1,396,427	3,391,737	2,793,668	7,581,832	6,426,860	795,712	359,260
1893 ..	1,371,389	3,433,627	2,409,187	7,214,203	6,109,910	752,415	351,878
1894 ..	1,332,669	3,472,253	2,359,030	7,163,952	6,106,197	736,741	321,014
1895 ..	1,321,541	3,538,942	2,153,059	7,013,542	5,976,282	713,495	323,765
1896 ..	1,389,473	3,524,102	2,452,542	7,366,117	6,257,022	765,155	353,940
1897 ..	1,430,561	3,684,880	3,133,221	8,248,662	6,990,939	856,706	401,017

TABLE IV.

(Tables prepared by Association of Municipal Corporations for Royal Commission on Local Taxation.)

A. EXCHEQUER CONTRIBUTIONS TO COUNTY BOROUGHS AND AMOUNTS PAID TO GUARDIANS OUT OF SUMS RECEIVED BY CORPORATION FROM LOCAL TAXATION ACCOUNT.

City or Borough.	Gross Amount received from Local Taxation Licenses, Probate Duty, Grant and Estate Duty.*	Amount thereof paid by Corporation to Guardians.	Amount received from Residue of Duties under Local Taxation (Customs and Excise) Act, 1890.	City or Borough.	Gross Amount received from Local Taxation Licenses, Probate Duty, Grant and Estate Duty.*	Amount thereof paid by Corporation to Guardians.	Amount received from Residue of Duties under Local Taxation (Customs and Excise) Act, 1890.
Barrow-in-Furness	£5,521	£1,617	£1,205	Manchester	£100,419	£39,923	£14,469
				Middlesbro'	8,420	3,586	944
Bath	8,431	3,504	1,509	Newport, Mon	9,154	2,475	1,349
Birkenhead	14,069	5,108	2,360	Norwich	13,848	6,310	1,511
Birmingham	78,251	35,026	11,083	Nottingham	31,726	11,695	4,248
Blackburn	11,295	3,700	2,150				
Bolton	12,665	4,937	2,121	Oldham	11,936	4,179	2,420
Bootle	10,179	5,692	2,121				
Bradford	27,050	9,450	5,271	Plymouth	11,438	3,959	1,592
Brighton	23,080	11,113	3,268	Portsmouth	22,344	10,794	3,217
Burnley	6,776	2,683	1,407	Preston	10,730	3,841	1,745
Bury	7,712	4,404	1,263				
				Reading	10,004	3,989	1,415
Canterbury	3,811	1,491	553	Rochdale	8,481	3,330	1,350
Chester	6,103	2,068	841	St. Helens	7,347	2,871	1,446
Coventry	5,977	2,379	845	Sheffield	44,422	16,358	5,642
				Southampton	12,467	4,510	1,533
Derby	13,807	4,943	1,912	South Shields	7,853	2,475	1,139
Devonport	6,570	2,387	955	Sunderland	16,821	6,516	2,092
				Swansea	12,577	3,361	1,167
Gateshead	9,740	3,563	1,092	Walsall	7,837	3,020	931
Gloucester	4,240	1,713	912	Wigan	5,543	1,684	858
Grimsby	4,486	866	751	Wol'hampton	11,716	5,310	1,421
				Worcester	8,516	2,579	947
Halifax	10,700	3,350	1,645				
Hanley	8,474	2,892	936	York	8,030	1,919	1,051
Huddersfield	13,722	3,404	1,962				
Hull	27,262	8,524	3,134	Grand Total for 47 English and Welsh Co. Boroughs	£730,359	£279,638	£105,653
Leicester	22,878	8,715	3,127				
Lincoln	4,975	1,419	734				

* Excluding costs of revising barristers' and election petitions.

TABLE IV.—*Continued.*

B. EXCHEQUER CONTRIBUTIONS TO NON-COUNTY BOROUGHS—AMOUNTS RECEIVED FROM COUNTY COUNCILS UNDER LOCAL GOVERNMENT ACT, 1888, AND LOCAL TAXATION (CUSTOMS AND EXCISE) ACT, 1890.

City or Borough.	Amount received from County Council under Local Government Act, 1888.	Amount received from County Council under Local Taxation (Customs & Excise) Act, 1890.	City or Borough.	Amount received from County Council under Local Government Act, 1888.	Amount received from County Council under Local Taxation (Customs & Excise) Act, 1890.
Ashton-under-Lyne	£3,045	£619	Kidwelly	£60	..
Bacup	4,420	257	King's Lynn	2,492	£374
Banbury	1,200	500	Lancaster	1,496	421
Barnsley	1,028	..	Leamington Spa	2,655	530
Bedford	2,295	..	Lewes	783	168
Berwick-upon-Tweed	2,108		Longton	1,683	239
Beverley	168	253	Loughborough	964	103
Bishop's Castle	358	..	Ludlow	188	..
Blackpool	715	476	Luton	3,448	350
Boston	1,605	..	Lydd	100	..
Brighouse	..	..	Lyme Regis	495	..
Burslem	3,626	4,162	Macclesfield	1,868	2,323
Calne	28	446	Maidstone	4,208	2,600
Cambridge	8,557	..	Maldon	..	..
Carmarthen	859	..	Middleton	2,531	195
Chatham	2,351	780	Montgomery	..	..
Cheltenham	2,209	850	Mossley	1,445	170
Chesterfield	2,432	182	Neath	531	25
Chichester	95	90	Nelson	1,035	230
Chorley	6	230	Newcastle-Under-Lyme	..	..
Christchurch	540	..	Ossett	..	..
Colne	1,975	170	Pembroke	910	..
Congleton	1,399	1,975	Peterborough	1,624	..
Conway	68	..	Rawtenstall	3,375	332
Crewe	2,712	513	Reigate	3,302	..
Darwen	2,129	357	Richmond Yorks	100	..
Daventry	567	..	Ripon	292	..
Denbigh	30	..	Sandwich	468	..
Dewsbury	295	..	Scarborough	2,098	1,100
Doncaster	2,260	..	Shrewsbury	2,896	..
Dover	4,421	865	Southport	4,042	719
Dunstable	353	100	Southwold	23	..
Durham	735	..	Stalybridge	1,924	- 100
Eastbourne	3,539	711	Stafford	260	169
East Retford	1,109	..	Stoke-on-Trent	2,300	198
Eccles	1,867	340	Tenby	223	..
Faversham	55	218	Thornaby-on-Tees	..	..
Glastonbury	751	..	Tiverton	2,264	..
Godalming	710	13	Todmorden	..	..
Guildford	1,559	73	Torquay	1,100	..
Harrogate	2,100	..	Tunbridge Wells	6,219	582
Haslingden	2,735	204	Wakefield	2,188	..
Hertford	102	185	Warrington	2,930	412
Heywood	2,636	289	Wisbech	35	..
Huntingdon	302	..	Wrexham	570	114
Hyde	1,892	586			
Kendal	1,382	..			
Kidderminster	2,048	..			

TABLE V.

(Tables handed in by Mr. John Richmond Cooper, Town Clerk of the County Borough of Walsall [see Minutes of Evidence, Vol. I., Questions 10,179—10,292] to Royal Commission on Local Taxation.

STATEMENT showing the RESULTS of the APPORTIONMENT of the LOCAL TAXATION LICENSES and PROBATE DUTY GRANT and ESTATE DUTY between COUNTIES and COUNTY BOROUGHS in ENGLAND and WALES in the year ended 31st March, 1806.

A. ADMINISTRATIVE COUNTIES.*

Counties receiving an Amount in Excess of their Contributions.		Counties receiving Less than they Contribute.	
County.	Amount of Excess.	County.	Amount of Deficiency.
	£ s. d.		£ s. d.
Chester	1,614 15 2	Berkshire..	258 16 7
Derby	1,278 11 1	Essex	4,798 15 1
Devon	356 6 6	Lancaster..	13,601 17 10
Durham	415 6 0	Leicester	450 5 11
Gloucester	3,363 3 10	Monmouth	177 12 11
Kent	1,200 13 7	Warwick	3,478 17 6
Lincoln (Lindsey) ..	3,354 4 6	York (West Riding) ..	4,809 8 11
Norfolk	4,422 10 9	Glamorgan	571 17 7
Northampton	2,401 5 6		
Northumberland ..	2,941 11 11		
Notts	821 19 2		
Oxford	766 1 7		
Somerset	2,067 16 10		
Stafford	1,608 8 5		
Suffolk (East)	597 16 2		
Sussex (East)	860 9 0		
York (East Riding) ..	1,210 3 1		
York (North Riding) ..	838 18 0		
Total	£30,120 1 1	Total	£23,147 12 4

* The counties of Southampton, Surrey, and Worcester, received the same amounts as were contributed by them.

TABLE V.—*Continued.*

STATEMENT showing the RESULTS of the APPORTIONMENT of the LOCAL TAXATION LICENSES and PROBATE DUTY GRANT and ESTATE DUTY between COUNTIES and COUNTY BOROUGHS in ENGLAND and WALES in the year ended 31st March, 1896—*continued.*

B. COUNTY BOROUGHS.*

County Boroughs receiving an Amount in Excess of their Contributions.		County Boroughs receiving Less than they Contribute.	
County Borough.	Amount of Excess.	County Borough.	Amount of Deficiency.
	£ s. D.		£ s. D.
Barrow-in-Furness ..	40 9 10	Bath	2,070 6 9
Birkenhead	976 7 11	Blackburn	4,333 10 7
Birmingham	6,731 6 11	Bolton	2,079 17 11
Bootle	4,281 14 7	Burnley	1,797 5 6
Bradford	2,365 1 4	Bury	394 12 11
Brighton	655 1 0	Canterbury	1,200 13 7
Bristol	12 9 5	Chester	1,932 16 9
Cardiff	1,864 16 5	Coventry .. ., ..	3,252 9 5
Devonport	599 15 7	Derby	1,273 11 1
Gateshead..	662 12 2	Exeter	343 16 2
Hanley	1,014 10 1	Gloucester	3,373 3 4
Halifax	518 13 10	Great Grimsby	1,821 2 3
Huddersfield	952 16 2	Great Yarmouth.. ..	635 10 3
Leeds	330 17 5	Hastings	1,515 10 0
Leicester	450 5 11	Ipswich	597 16 2
Liverpool	2,037 8 3	Kingston-upon-Hull ..	62 5 6
Manchester	23,058 5 0	Lincoln	1,533 2 3
Middlesbrough	329 7 9	Newcastle-upon-Tyne ..	2,941 11 11
Newport (Mon.).. ..	177 12 11	Northampton	2,401 5 6
Reading	258 10 7	Norwich	3,787 0 6
Salford	7,618 14 2	Nottingham	821 19 2
Sheffield	1,098 3 8	Oldham	3,257 4 7
Sunderland	404 18 10	Oxford	766 1 7
West Bromwich.. ..	746 9 1	Plymouth..	612 5 11
West Ham	4,798 15 1	Preston	4,503 5 0
		Rochdale	1,920 6 4
		South Shields	1,482 17 0
		St. Helens	1,629 4 9
		Stockport	1,101 11 1
		Swansea	1,292 18 10
		Walsall	1,672 12 7
		Wigan	3,076 1 0
		Wolverhampton.. ..	1,696 15 0
		York	2,772 11 10
Total	£61,935 15 0	Total	£63,958 3 9

* The county boroughs of Portsmouth, Southampton, Croydon, Dudley, and Worcester received the same amounts as were contributed by them.

TABLE VI.

(Tables handed in by Mr. J. R. Cooper to the Royal Commission on Local Taxation.)

STATEMENT showing the TOTAL AMOUNTS and the AMOUNTS per HEAD RECEIVED by certain COUNTIES and COUNTY BOROUGHS in ENGLAND and WALES from the RESIDUE of the PROCEEDS of the LOCAL TAXATION (CUSTOMS and EXCISE) DUTIES in the year ended 31st March, 1896.

A. ADMINISTRATIVE COUNTIES.

County	Population, 1891.	Share of Residue of Proceeds of Customs and Excise Duties distributed in same manner as English share of Local Taxation Probate Duty.	Amount Paid to each County Council.	
			Total Amount.	Amount per Head.
		£ s. D.	£ s. D.	Pence.
Durham	721,481	12,913 0 11	13,619 13 2	4·5
Cornwall	322,571	6,873 11 7	6,873 11 7	5·1
Staffordshire	818,290	16,061 12 7	17,727 3 1	5·1
East Suffolk ..	133,478	3,833 7 6	4,059 5 2	5·3
Yorks (West Riding) ..	1,351,570	30,734 1 9	30,506 16 0	5·4
Derbyshire..	426,768	9,997 18 7	9,975 5 3	5·6
Hampshire	386,849	9,039 0 5	9,039 0 5	5·6
Monmouthshire	203,347	4,372 6 0	4,781 1 7	5·6
Lancashire..	1,768,273	40,485 16 5	42,443 3 0	5·7
Cumberland	266,549	6,330 11 8	6,330 11 8	5·7
Yorks (North Riding) ..	284,837	6,824 13 7	7,160 14 11	6·0
Northumberland	319,730	7,881 7 9	8,003 6 11	6·0
Nottinghamshire.. ..	231,946	5,802 13 1	5,988 0 4	6·1
Leicestershire	200,468	5,485 13 5	5,201 1 8	6·2
Devon	455,353	12,120 8 11	12,255 10 11	6·4
West Sussex .. .	140,619	3,779 18 7	3,779 18 7	6·4
Westmorland	66,098	1,792 14 9	1,792 14 9	6·5
Cheshire	536,644	14,510 3 10	14,997 5 7	6·5
Worcestershire	296,661	8,557 8 7	8,557 8 7	6·9
East Sussex	240,264	8,113 13 1	7,102 0 10	7·0
Bedfordshire	160,704	4,770 2 3	4,770 2 3	7·1
Salop	236,339	7,159 11 6	7,159 11 6	7·2
Norfolk	317,983	9,064 6 5	9,596 7 0	7·2
Cambridgeshire	121,961	3,696 12 7	3,696 12 7	7·2
Warwickshire	307,193	8,518 15 4	9,410 8 8	7·3
Essex	579,355	18,073 15 6	18,077 19 1	7·4
Northamptonshire ..	203,247	6,187 0 4	6,358 8 2	7·5
Hertfordshire	224,550	7,034 4 0	7,034 4 0	7·5
Kent..	785,674	24,634 18 4	24,570 12 9	7·5
Lindsey (Lincs.)	199,055	6,354 9 3	6,236 18 11	7·5
Berkshire	176,109	5,789 0 2	5,672 19 4	7·7
Oxfordshire	145,449	¯5,099 6 5	4,795 11 11	7·9
Somerset	386,866	13,237 2 9	13,198 15 2	8·1
Dorset	194,517	6,778 12 6	6,778 12 6	8·3
Wiltshire	264,997	10,123 17 5	10,123 17 5	9·1
Surrey	418,856	16,172 14 5	16,172 14 5	9·2
London	4,232,118	178,558 7 4	178,558 7 4	10·1

TABLE VI.—*Continued.*

Statement showing the Total Amounts and the Amounts per Head received by certain Counties and County Boroughs in England and Wales from the Residue of the Proceeds of the Local Taxation (Customs and Excise) Duties in the year ended 31st March, 1896—*continued.*

B. COUNTY BOROUGHS.

County Borough.	Population, 1891.	Share of Residue of Proceeds of Customs and Excise Duties distributed in same manner as English share of Local Taxation Probate Duty.	Amount Paid to each Borough Council. Total Amount.	Amount per Head.
		£ s. d.	£ s. d.	Pence.
Walsall	71,789	1,082 5 11	931 2 10	3·1
Norwich	100,970	1,999 19 8	1,510 12 5	3·5
Northampton	61,012	1,079 14 9	908 6 11	3·5
Kingston-on-Hull	200,044	4,577 18 7	3,134 8 0	3·7
Coventry	52,724	897 4 5	845 0 4	3·8
Stockport	70,263	1,967 0 2	1,170 3 1	3·9
West Bromwich	95,474	1,070 1 5	1,010 7 1	4·0
Wolverhampton	82,662	1,022 8 11	1,421 0 11	4·1
Blackburn	120,064	1,913 11 2	2,149 12 7	4·2
Hanley	54,946	1,289 5 2	936 0 1	4·3
Bolton	115,002	2,278 0 5	2,120 14 3	4·4
Rochdale	71,401	1,506 14 11	1,349 10 10	4·5
Nottingham	213,877	4,433 15 11	4,248 8 8	4·7
Portsmouth	159,251	3,217 6 4	3,217 6 4	4·8
St. Helens	71,288	1,090 10 9	1,445 18 10	4·8
Worcester	42,908	947 5 1	947 5 1	5·2
Birmingham	478,113	11,922 17 3	11,083 8 0	5·5
Manchester	505,368	13,959 16 1	14,469 0 9	6·8
Bath	51,844	1,349 4 10	1,509 3 10	6·9
Oxford	45,742	1,148 10 8	1,452 5 2	7·6
Liverpool	517,980	19,823 17 4	17,033 3 5	7·8
Bootle	49,217	1,393 17 6	2,120 14 3	10·3

TABLE VII.

*Memorandum by Mr. F. C. Hulton to the Royal Commission
on Local Taxation.*

TABLE showing the DISTRIBUTION between COUNTIES (including County Boroughs deemed
to be situate therein) of the PROBATE DUTY GRANT and ESTATE DUTY for Year ending
31st March, 1896, on the Basis of DISCONTINUED GRANTS (Local Government Act, 1888,
Section 22) and the effect of distribution according to RATEABLE VALUE at LADY DAY,
1895.

(See Minutes of Evidence, Vol. I., Questions 6014-6026, 6030-6037, 6046-6048, 6057-6059.*)*

Name of County.	Share of discontinued Grants, received during Year ending 31st March, 1888.	Share of Probate Duty Grant and Estate Duty for Year ending 31st March, 1896.	Distribution according to Rateable Value.			
			Rateable Value (Poor Rate) of Counties (including County Boroughs deemed to be situate therein), March, 1895.	Share of Probate Duty Grant and Estate Duty supposing Distribution had been according to Rateable Value at Lady Day, 1895.	Effect. Increase (+) or Decrease (−).	
					Actual Amount.	Percentage Amount.
ENGLAND.	£	£	£	£		
Bedford	16,779	10,640	826,392	9,207	− 1,433	− 13·5
Berkshire ..	24,932	15,809	1,428,800	15,919	+ 110	+ ·7
Buckingham ..	20,676	13,111	1,167,949	13,012	− 99	− ·8
Cambridge ..	13,003	8,245	685,514	7,637	− 608	− 7·4
Cheshire ..	68,935	43,712	4,070,871	45,355	+ 1,643	+ 3·8
Cornwall ..	24,178	15,331	1,309,788	14,593	− 738	− 4·8
Cumberland ..	22,268	14,120	1,605,480	17,887	+ 3,767	+ 26·7
Derby	41,814	26,514	2,525,901	28,142	+ 1,628	+ 6·1
Devon	55,986	35,501	3,245,289	36,157	+ 656	+ 1·8
Dorset	23,844	15,119	1,058,800	11,796	− 3,323	− 22·0
Durham	63,115	40,021	4,287,160	47,764	+ 7,743	+ 19·3
Ely, Isle of ..	8,045	5,101	431,311	4,805	− 296	− 5·8
Essex	81,691	51,800	3,816,088	42,516	− 9,284	− 17·9
* Gloucester ..	69,735	44,219	3,282,704	36,573	− 7,646	− 17·3
Hereford ..	18,772	11,903	885,959	9,871	− 2,032	− 17·1
Hertford ..	24,743	15,690	1,343,942	14,973	− 717	− 4·6
Huntingdon ..	7,473	4,739	404,783	4,510	− 229	− 4·8
Kent	83,374	56,038	4,599,823	51,248	− 4,790	− 8·5
Lancaster ..	337,083	213,744	19,487,828	217,119	+ 3,375	+ 1·6
Leicester ..	29,295	18,576	1,981,754	22,079	+ 3,503	+ 18·9
Lincoln	47,737	30,270	2,958,533	32,962	+ 2,692	+ 8·9
London	628,084	398,267	34,457,948	383,904	− 14,363	− 3·6
Middlesex ..	80,397	50,980	3,394,406	37,818	− 13,162	− 25·8
Monmouth ..	21,561	13,672	1,199,342	13,362	− 310	− 2·3
Norfolk	42,118	26,707	2,287,264	25,483	− 1,224	− 4·6
Northampton ..	25,561	16,208	1,423,996	15,865	− 343	− 2·1
Northumberland	42,228	26,777	2,929,227	32,635	+ 5,858	+ 21·9
Nottingham ..	36,007	22,832	2,244,809	25,010	+ 2,178	+ 9·5
Oxford	21,977	13,936	1,052,044	11,721	− 2,215	− 15·9
Peterborough ..	3,567	2,262	217,359	2,422	+ 160	+ 7·1
Rutland ..	2,718	1,723	181,576	2,023	+ 300	+ 17·4

* Bristol county borough is in the counties of Gloucester and Somerset, but in the returns
of the local taxation account it is treated as in Gloucester.

TABLE VII.—*continued.*

Name of County.	Share of discontinued Grants, received during Year ending 31st March, 1888.	Share of Probate Duty Grant and Estate Duty for Year ending 31st March, 1896.	Distribution according to Rateable Value.			
			Rateable Value (Poor Rate) of Counties (including County Boroughs deemed to be situate therein), March, 1895.	Share of Probate Duty Grant and Estate Duty supposing Distribution had been according to Rateable Value at Lady Day, 1895.	Effect. Increase (+) or Decrease (—).	
					Actual Amount.	Percentage Amount.
ENGLAND—*continued.*	£	£	£	£	£	
Salop	25,184	15,969	1,610,089	17,938	+ 1,969	+ 12·3
*Somerset ..	51,308	32,534	2,880,755	32,095	— 439	— 1·3
Southampton ..	48,505	30,757	2,979,142	33,191	+ 2,434	+ 7·9
Stafford	77,476	49,127	4,434,692	49,408	+ 281	— ·6
Suffolk	25,902	16,424	1,680,455	18,722	+ 2,298	+ 14·0
Surrey	70,448	44,671	3,598,260	40,089	— 4,582	— 10·3
Sussex	55,436	35,152	3,497,190	38,963	+ 3,811	+ 10·8
Warwick ..	75,060	47,595	4,116,949	45,868	— 1,727	— 3·6
Westmorland ..	6,306	3,999	534,816	5,959	+ 1,960	+ 49·0
Wight, Isle of ..	9,062	5,746	432,632	4,820	— 926	— 16·1
Wilts	35,611	22,581	1,435,121	15,989	— 6,592	— 29·2
Worcester ..	36,418	23,093	1,859,432	20,716	— 2,377	— 10·3
York, East ..	28,118	17,830	1,936,314	21,573	+ 3,743	+ 21·0
York, North ..	28,196	17,879	2,298,979	25,613	+ 7,734	+ 43·3
York, West ..	181,285	114,953	10,844,494	120,821	+ 5,868	+ 5·1
York, County Borough ..	3,955	2,508	244,095	2,720	+ 212	+ 8·5
WALES.						
Anglesey ..	2,516	1,595	211,787	2,360	+ 765	+ 48·0
Brecon	5,136	3,257	276,971	3,086	— 171	— 5·3
Cardigan ..	4,396	2,787	234,854	2,617	— 170	— 6·1
Carmarthen ..	9,107	5,775	585,812	6,527	+ 752	+ 13·0
Carnarvon ..	8,354	5,297	474,182	5,283	— 14	— ·3
Denbigh ..	10,923	6,926	591,346	6,588	— 338	— 4·9
Flint	7,829	4,964	431,765	4,810	— 154	— 3·1
Glamorgan ..	41,345	26,217	3,661,935	40,799	+ 14,582	+ 55·6
Merioneth ..	3,788	2,402	234,276	2,610	+ 208	+ 8·7
Montgomery ..	7,545	4,784	366,594	4,084	— 700	— 14·6
Pembroke ..	5,787	3,670	395,405	4,405	+ 735	+ 20·0
Radnor	2,692	1,707	156,537	1,744	+ 37	+ 2·2
Total, (Eng. and Wales), ..	2,860,384	1,813,766	162,797,519	1,813,766	—	—

* Bristol county borough is in the counties of Gloucester and Somerset, but in the returns of the local taxation account it is treated as in Gloucester.

Printed by Cowan & Co., Limited, Perth.

www.ingramcontent.com/pod-product-compliance
Lightning Source LLC
Chambersburg PA
CBHW030600270326
41927CB00007B/984